BEYOND THE WELCOME MAT

CREATING CULTURALLY COMPETENT EXPERIENCES IN HOSPITALITY AND TOURISM

DR. LAMONT "MONTEE" EVANS

moja Publishing, LLC
www.mojapublishing.com

Copyright © 2024 by LaMont Evans.

All rights reserved. No part of this book may be used or reproduced in any form whatsoever without written permission except in the case of brief quotations in critical articles or reviews.

Printed in the United States of America.

For more information, contact us via email or visit our website:

E : admin@beyondthewelcomemat.com

https://www.beyondthewelcomemat.com

Cover design by Nathaniel Ashie (Ghana, West Africa)

ISBN – Paperback : 979-8-9853428-3-3

ISBN – Hardcover : 979-8-9853428-4-0

ISBN – eBook : 979-8-9853428-5-7

First Edition: November 2024

TABLE OF CONTENTS

CHAPTER 1 : A HISTORICAL CONTEXT OF DIVERSITY IN HOSPITALITY AND TOURISM 5

CHAPTER 2: CULTURAL COMPETENCE: WHAT IT IS AND WHY IT MATTERS 12

CHAPTER 3: THE STATE OF DIVERSITY TODAY: NUMBERS AND NARRATIVES 22

CHAPTER 4: THE BUSINESS ADVANTAGE OF DIVERSITY, EQUITY, AND INCLUSION 32

CHAPTER 5: CULTURAL COMPETENCE IN ACTION: BEST PRACTICIES AND STRATEGIES 41

CHAPTER 6: CREATING A DIVERSE FUTURE FOR THE HOSPITALITY & TOURISM INDUSTRY 51

CHAPTER 7: BUILDING PARTNERSHIPS FOR A DIVERSE INDUSTRY 62

CHAPTER 8: BREAKING BARRIERS AND REDEFINING NARRATIVES 73

CHAPTER 9: PREPARING FOR A GLOBAL MARKET: EMBRACING CULTURAL COMPETENCE IN A CHANGING WORLD 84

CHAPTER 10: PITBULL CONVENTION & CONFERENCE SERVICES: LEADING THE WAY 96

CONCLUSION: CHARTING THE PATH FORWARD FOR AN INCLUSIVE HOSPITALITY & TOURISM INDUSTRY 111

ABOUT THE AUTHOR 120

ACKNOWLEDGMENTS 122

CHAPTER 1

A HISTORICAL CONTEXT OF DIVERSITY IN HOSPITALITY AND TOURISM

To understand the state of diversity, equity and inclusion in today's hospitality and tourism industry, we must first step back and explore how the industry has evolved over time. This is a story marked by both progress and setbacks, where access and opportunities for people of color have ebbed and flowed based on the social, economic, and political climates of the times.

The Segregated Beginnings

The history of hospitality and tourism in the United States is tightly interwoven with the country's racial dynamics. During the early 20th century, hotels, restaurants, and travel services were deeply segregated, and African Americans, *in particular*, were often denied access to basic accommodations and services. **The Green Book**, a travel guide published from 1936 to 1966, became a crucial resource for Black travelers who faced widespread discrimination. This annual guide listed hotels, restaurants, and other establishments where they would be welcomed and safe.

The very existence of the Green Book underscores how exclusionary the hospitality and tourism industry was at the time, effectively closing the door to a significant segment of the population. Businesses, largely operated by and for white patrons, saw little need to diversify or cater to people of color. Even in cities with substantial Black populations, hotel accommodations were often segregated, and it wasn't until the Civil Rights Movement of the 1960s that legal barriers began to fall.

Yet, while the laws changed, attitudes and practices did not always follow suit. Many hospitality and tourism businesses were slow to hire people of color into positions of influence and leadership. This historical context still affects the industry today, with many establishments remaining predominantly white-owned and operated, even in areas with diverse clientele.

The Tourism Boom and Shifts in the Industry

The post-World War II era saw the rise of middle-class travel and a booming tourism industry. However, the benefits of this growth were not equally distributed. Large hotel chains, convention & visitor bureaus (CVBs), and destination marketing organizations (DMOs) were primarily focused on attracting white travelers, often leaving communities of color out of the conversation. Marketing materials often depicted a singular vision of leisure and luxury that did not reflect the diversity of travelers who wished to enjoy these experiences.

As the industry expanded, there was an assumption that the services and experiences provided would cater to all, regardless of race, ethnicity, or culture. However, this one-size-fits-all approach often resulted in a disconnect between businesses and their increasingly diverse customer base. Without diverse voices at the table to inform planning and marketing strategies, many travelers of color felt—and continue to feel—excluded or overlooked.

Pioneers of Change and the Fight for Inclusion

Despite these challenges, there have always been trailblazers who fought to create more inclusive spaces within the industry. One key figure was **Doctor John Somerville**, an African American entrepreneur who, in the mid-20th century, became one of the first Black owners of a major hotel, the *Dunbar Hotel* in Los Angeles. The Dunbar was more than just a place for Black travelers to find accommodation; it was a cultural hub where prominent Black entertainers, politicians, and community leaders gathered and connected.

Somerville's success showed the power and potential of creating spaces that catered to African Americans. The

Dunbar became a symbol of what was possible when the hospitality and tourism industry embraced diversity, and it set the stage for future African American entrepreneurs to enter the industry.

Similarly, in the mid-1980s, Harvard Law School alumnus **Reginald F. Lewis** founded *TLC Beatrice International*, becoming one of the first African Americans to own a billion-dollar multinational corporation. His success in breaking racial and business barriers inspired a new generation of Black entrepreneurs to pursue opportunities in hospitality, tourism, and related fields. Lewis was the first African American ever to close an overseas billion dollar leveraged buyout deal.

Challenges of the Modern Era

While there have been strides in increasing diversity and representation in the industry, challenges remain. Many hospitality and tourism businesses still struggle with *hiring* diverse staff, *fostering* inclusive work environments, and *creating* marketing campaigns that authentically represent different cultures. In particular, senior leadership roles in hotels, CVBs, and DMOs remain predominantly white, which perpetuates a cycle where diverse voices are not considered or included in decision-making processes.

One example is the lack of Black executives in the hotel industry. In 2021, a survey by the Castell Project found that only **2% of hotel industry executives** at the director through

CEO level on company websites were Black, a startling figure given the diversity of the overall hospitality workforce. This disparity highlights the disconnect between the industry's front-line diversity and its leadership ranks. It raises questions about pathways to leadership, access to opportunities, and the commitment of the industry to truly embrace diversity.

Missed Opportunities and the Business Case for Diversity

The lack of diversity isn't just a social issue; it's a *business issue*. According to a 2020 study by McKinsey & Company, companies in the top quartile for ethnic and cultural diversity in executive teams were **36% more likely** to have above-average profitability compared to those in the bottom quartile. For the hospitality and tourism industry, this means that embracing diversity is not just about social justice—**it's a smart business move** that can drive growth, enhance brand reputation, and attract a broader customer base.

One notable example is **Marriott International**, which has made concerted efforts in recent years to increase its diversity, equity, and inclusion efforts. The company established a global diversity and inclusion council, set goals for supplier diversity, and invested in training and development programs aimed at creating a more inclusive workforce. This proactive approach has positioned Marriott as a leader in the industry, showcasing how businesses can benefit from intentional and strategic efforts toward diversity, equity, and inclusion.

Conclusion: Understanding the Path Forward

The history of diversity in hospitality and tourism is complex and layered. While there has been progress, there are still significant barriers to full representation and inclusion. Understanding where the industry has been helps us to see where it needs to go—and how we can all play a role in that journey. By embracing diversity, fostering cultural competence, and listening to the voices of those who have been marginalized, the hospitality and tourism industry can create richer, more meaningful experiences for all.

As you move forward in this book, I will explore how these historical dynamics continue to shape today's industry and discuss practical steps for building a more diverse and culturally competent hospitality and tourism future. It's a journey worth taking, and one that will ultimately benefit everyone involved.

References:

1. **Green Book** – The Negro Motorist Green Book: Victor Hugo Green.

2. **Castell Project Study** (2021) – *"Black Representation in Hospitality Leadership."*

3. **McKinsey & Company Study** (2020) – *"Diversity Wins: How Inclusion Matters."*

4. **Marriott International's Diversity and Inclusion Efforts** – Company reports and diversity initiatives.

CHAPTER 2

CULTURAL COMPETENCE: WHAT IT IS AND WHY IT MATTERS

In the hospitality and tourism industry, diversity is more than just hiring a mix of people from different backgrounds or showing diverse faces in advertisements. To truly serve a global and multifaceted clientele, businesses must also develop cultural competence—*the ability to understand, respect, and appropriately respond to the cultural differences and needs of their guests and employees.* Without it, the potential to connect authentically with travelers is lost, and opportunities to build meaningful and profitable relationships are overlooked.

Defining Cultural Competence in Hospitality and Tourism

Cultural competence goes beyond basic diversity initiatives. It's a deeper, more intentional approach that emphasizes understanding and embracing the unique values, customs, and behaviors of different cultures. It requires a willingness to learn, adapt, and, most importantly, create an environment where guests and employees feel seen, respected, and valued for who they are.

In hospitality and tourism, cultural competence is vital because the industry is about creating experiences—experiences that cater to people's needs, preferences, and worldviews. Travelers come with a set of expectations shaped by their cultural backgrounds, and understanding those expectations is key to delivering a positive experience. Whether it's knowing that *certain foods* or *gestures* have different meanings in different cultures or understanding religious practices, cultural competence equips staff and organizations to make every guest feel at home.

The Importance of Cultural Competence for Global Travelers

In an increasingly globalized world, travelers expect more than just a bed to sleep in or a convention center to meet in—they expect experiences that respect and celebrate their identities. For example, a Muslim traveler might be looking for hotels that accommodate Halal dietary requirements and offer privacy for prayer. An LGBTQ+ traveler may prioritize destinations and establishments that are openly welcoming and affirming of their identities. And a family traveling from Japan might be accustomed to certain cultural norms around hospitality that differ significantly from Western practices.

A lack of cultural competence can result in lost business opportunities, misunderstandings, and, worse, negative experiences that drive guests away. On the other hand, a commitment to learning and understanding these cultural nuances can create exceptional experiences that build customer loyalty and generate positive word-of-mouth.

Hilton's Guest Experience Focus:

For instance, Hilton has adopted a *"hospitality for all"* ethos by ensuring that services are culturally sensitive and accessible. The Hilton Honors program caters to loyal guests worldwide and is customized to address various preferences, including dietary needs (*e.g., Halal, Kosher, Vegetarian*), language support, and cultural events. Staff members are trained on culturally competent guest service, such as acknowledging and respecting different communication styles and traditions, offering a personalized approach to a diverse clientele.

Cultural Competence within the Workforce

Cultural competence isn't just about serving guests—it's also crucial for creating inclusive, supportive environments for a diverse workforce. The hospitality and tourism industry is one of the most diverse in terms of front-line staff. From hotel housekeepers and chefs to tour guides and concierges, employees often come from various racial, ethnic, cultural, and socioeconomic backgrounds. However, this diversity is often not reflected in management and leadership roles, creating a disconnect between those who provide the services and those who make the decisions.

Hilton's Team Member Resource Groups (TMRGs):

Hilton's TMRGs play a significant role in fostering cultural competence and support for employees. These groups—such as **Hilton Pride** for LGBTQ+ employees, **Abilities in Motion** for those with disabilities, and **Women's Resource Group**—allow staff to connect based on shared cultural experiences and serve as advisory groups that help the company shape policies and guest experiences. By valuing diverse voices, Hilton ensures that its internal culture and external services reflect a broad range of perspectives.

Hyatt's Employee Engagement through Business Resource Groups (BRGs):

Similarly, Hyatt has established BRGs like **Hyatt Mosaic** to support multicultural inclusion and ensure that employee insights influence the company's practices and policies. These resource groups help enhance the cultural competence of the brand and empower staff to provide better service to guests from diverse backgrounds.

Localized Cultural Competence in Guest Experience

Cultural competence often requires localizing services to meet the needs of regional guests, and both **DoubleTree by**

Hilton and **InterContinental Hotels Group** (IHG) have adopted this practice effectively.

DoubleTree's Warm Cookie Welcome and Global Adaptations:

DoubleTree's signature cookie welcome is a gesture that fosters warmth and hospitality for all guests. To ensure inclusivity, the hotel offers allergen-free and vegan cookie options. This simple act of adapting to guests' dietary preferences showcases cultural competence. DoubleTree also localizes its services in Middle Eastern and Southeast Asian markets by providing private dining for families, Halal dietary options, and service adjustments during religious observances like Ramadan.

IHG's Culturally Tailored Services and Inclusive Guest Experience:

IHG has embraced cultural competence by customizing its guest experience to cater to different cultural preferences. For example, in properties targeting Asian travelers, InterContinental Hotels & Resorts offer Mandarin-speaking staff, provide traditional Chinese breakfast items, and respect dining customs. In the Middle East, IHG's properties accommodate religious observances by offering prayer rooms, special meal arrangements for Ramadan, and amenities that reflect local traditions.

Building Cultural Competence: Skills and Approaches

Developing cultural competence is an ongoing process that requires intention and effort. Here are some key skills and approaches that are crucial for businesses in the hospitality and tourism industry:

1. **Self-Awareness**: Understanding your own cultural background, biases, and worldviews is the first step toward building cultural competence. Hospitality and tourism professionals need to reflect on how their perspectives influence their interactions with both guests and colleagues.

2. **Curiosity and Willingness to Learn**: A culturally competent individual is constantly learning. This includes seeking out information on different cultures, traditions, and beliefs, as well as being open to new ways of doing things. For example, learning about common travel customs and preferences of different cultural groups can help personalize services and make guests feel more at ease.

3. **Active Listening and Empathy**: Cultural competence involves the ability to *listen* carefully to others, *understand* their perspectives, and *empathize* with their experiences. In the hospitality and tourism industry, this means <u>truly</u> listening to the needs and preferences of guests, even when they differ significantly from your own.

4. **Adaptability and Flexibility**: A hallmark of cultural competence is the ability to adapt your behavior and services to meet the needs of diverse guests. This could mean adjusting the menu to include vegetarian options for Indian travelers, offering spaces that are family-friendly for Middle Eastern guests who often travel in larger family groups, or training staff on how to respect different communication styles.

The Benefits of Cultural Competence for the Industry

Cultural competence has tangible benefits for businesses in the hospitality and tourism industry. It enhances the guest experience, increases customer satisfaction and loyalty, and helps organizations stand out in a competitive market. Moreover, it fosters a positive work environment, improving employee engagement and retention.

Ritz-Carlton's Personalized Service Philosophy:

Ritz-Carlton exemplifies cultural competence through its **Gold Standards** and personalized approach to guest service. Known for extensive training that includes understanding cultural preferences and customs, Ritz-Carlton staff provide experiences tailored to their global clientele, whether it's offering preferred bedding for Asian guests or organizing special in-room celebrations for travelers from Latin American cultures.

IHG Academy and Community Engagement:

IHG's **IHG Academy** partnerships with educational and community organizations offer skills training and work experience, with a particular focus on youth, women, and marginalized communities. By fostering cultural competence through these programs, IHG ensures a more inclusive workforce and creates staff that is better equipped to understand and serve guests from diverse backgrounds.

These examples show that cultural competence in the hospitality and tourism industry is not just about representation—it's about **building authentic connections** with both guests and employees, resulting in better experiences and greater business success. Authentic connections have a value which cannot be projected or estimated, it brings a level of loyalty no number-cruncher can provide.

Conclusion: The Path to Cultural Competence

Cultural competence is not a box to be checked but an ongoing journey that requires commitment, humility, and a genuine desire to create welcoming spaces for all. As the hospitality and tourism industry becomes more global and diverse, the importance of developing cultural competence will only continue to grow. It is a key differentiator for businesses that want to build meaningful connections, foster brand loyalty, and succeed in an ever-changing world.

By embracing these principles, the hospitality and tourism industry can create richer experiences, empower their diverse workforce, and leave a positive impact on the guests and communities they serve.

References:

1. **Ritz-Carlton's Cultural Competence** – Ritz-Carlton Gold Standards and Service Philosophy.

2. **Hilton's Diversity and Inclusion Efforts** – Hilton's Travel with Purpose and TMRGs.

3. **DoubleTree's Culturally Inclusive Services** – DoubleTree's localized adaptations and guest services.

4. **IHG's Global Diversity Strategy** – IHG Academy, Mosaic BRG, and InterContinental's culturally tailored services.

CHAPTER 3

THE STATE OF DIVERSITY TODAY: NUMBERS AND NARRATIVES

While there has been considerable conversation and growing awareness around diversity, equity, and inclusion in recent years, the hospitality and tourism industry still have significant strides to make. Despite the obvious benefits of a diverse workforce and the increasing need to cater to diverse guest experiences, **the data** often tells a different story. In this chapter, we will explore the current state of diversity in the hospitality and tourism industry, examine key statistics, and share narratives that reveal both progress and persistent challenges. Some of the data displays startling revelations around where we are today in hospitality and tourism.

Current Landscape: Representation and Disparities

The hospitality and tourism industry has a diverse workforce on the front lines, with employees from various racial, ethnic, cultural, gender, sexual orientation, and cultural backgrounds working as front-desk clerks, housekeepers, kitchen staff, and concierge services. However, **the further up** the ladder one climbs, *the less diverse* the representation becomes. Leadership positions in hotels, CVBs, and DMOs remain disproportionately filled by white professionals, with people of color and women often significantly underrepresented.

The Castell Project's 2021 Study provides a revealing snapshot of the disparities within the industry. As stated in a previous chapter, this study found that only **2% of executive roles in the hotel industry** were held by Black professionals, despite African American workers making up a much larger portion of the front-line workforce. This indicates a *"leaky pipeline"* where people of color are not advancing to leadership positions at the same rate as their white counterparts, resulting in a lack of diverse voices in decision-making processes. In many urban cities throughout America, I have witnessed people of color at the lower level (*non-decision-making roles*), but the leadership and management were white. This is not encouraging to staff who wish to work their way up the career ladder, because those at the top of the ladder don't look like them. Loyalty is compromised when people don't see themselves in positions higher than where they are.

Women also face a similar imbalance in leadership representation. While they make up a large portion of the hospitality workforce, particularly in front-line roles, they often struggle to reach executive positions. The same Castell Project study showed that women held only **12% of hospitality industry leadership roles**. The intersection of race and gender further complicates these disparities, with women of color experiencing even greater barriers to advancement.

Diverse Workforce, Homogeneous Leadership: Voices from the Industry

The gap between a diverse workforce and homogeneous leadership is one of the most glaring issues in hospitality and tourism. While hotels, CVBs, DMOs, and tourism companies often showcase their diverse teams on marketing materials, the reality is that people of color and women rarely hold the power to make critical decisions.

Voices from the Field:

Consider the experience of *Melanie*, an African American hotel manager based in Atlanta, who shared her story at a recent diversity forum. Despite years of experience and dedication, she noticed that many of her peers were promoted to executive roles, while she was passed over multiple times. *"It was like there was an invisible barrier that I could never break through,"* she explained. *"No matter how much experience or education I had, there was always a sense that leadership roles were for someone else."*

Similarly, *Jose*, a Latinx event planner in Los Angeles, faced challenges in bringing diverse perspectives into his work. *"Whenever I proposed events or partnerships with organizations from the Latinx community, I was often met with resistance or indifference,"* he noted. *"It was as if our culture wasn't seen as profitable or worth the effort, despite the significant contributions of Latinx communities to the city's tourism economy."*

These narratives are reflective of the broader struggles many people of color face in the industry—a lack of upward mobility, an absence of mentorship opportunities, and a feeling of exclusion from decision-making circles.

The Business Case for Diversity in Leadership

The lack of diversity in leadership is not just a social issue; it has real economic consequences. Studies have shown that companies with diverse leadership tend to outperform those with homogeneous teams, thanks to increased innovation, better decision-making, and a broader customer appeal.

A 2020 **McKinsey & Company study** revealed that companies in the top quartile for ethnic and cultural diversity on executive teams were **36% more likely** to achieve above-average profitability than companies in the bottom quartile. For gender diversity, the top-performing companies were **25% more likely** to achieve financial success. Diversity is directly tied to profitably in some instances.

The hospitality and tourism industry, in particular, stands to benefit greatly from diverse leadership. Hotels, restaurants, CVBs, DMOs, and event venues operate on the principle of understanding and serving a variety of guest needs and preferences. Without diverse voices in leadership, these organizations miss out on valuable insights and perspectives that could enhance customer experience and business performance. It's hard for management to understand cultural nuances when they have no diversity in the sales staff or leadership team.

Case Study: Marriott International's Diversity Efforts

Marriott International, one of the largest hotel chains in the world, and my personal favorite, is often cited as an industry leader in diversity, equity, and inclusion. The company's approach has been strategic, intentional, and data driven. Marriott has established a **Global Diversity and Inclusion Council**, set goals for supplier diversity, and invested in training programs aimed at building a more inclusive workforce. One key aspect of Marriott's strategy is its **emphasis on partnerships** with organizations like the **National Minority Supplier Development Council (NMSDC)** and the **Women's Business Enterprise National Council (WBENC)** to ensure diverse suppliers are given opportunities within the company's supply chain.

Moreover, Marriott has also focused on building a leadership pipeline for women and people of color. Through initiatives like the **Emerging Leaders Program**, Marriott provides mentorship, training, and networking opportunities to high-potential diverse employees, preparing them for senior leadership roles. The company's **Women's Leadership Development Initiative** similarly works to create pathways for women to move up the corporate ladder.

While there is still progress to be made, Marriott's approach to promoting diversity in leadership serves as a model for how the industry can take active steps to close representation gaps.

Narratives of Progress and Remaining Challenges

Though challenges persist, there are stories of progress and success across the hospitality and tourism industry. **Hilton's Commitment to Diversity** is another example. Ranked as one of the "Best Workplaces for Diversity" by *Fortune*, Hilton has made diversity, equity, and inclusion an integral part of its company culture. In addition to its **Team Member Resource Groups (TMRGs)**, Hilton has developed leadership programs aimed at promoting diverse talent within the company, and its executive team reflects a commitment to gender and racial inclusion.

At the same time, brands like **IHG (InterContinental Hotels Group)** have taken a proactive approach to cultural competence by implementing **IHG Academy**, providing skills training and employment opportunities to diverse and underrepresented communities. IHG's work through

Employee Resource Groups (ERGs) ensures that diverse perspectives are represented in policies, guest services, and marketing strategies.

The Power of Storytelling: Sharing Diverse Perspectives

Storytelling plays a crucial role in understanding the state of diversity today. By sharing stories of success and challenges faced by people of color and women in the hospitality and tourism industry, a space for reflection and change can be created. For example:

- **The Story of the Westin Denver International Airport Hotel**: This hotel was recognized for its efforts to create a more inclusive work environment by providing cultural competence training to all staff and offering opportunities for front-line employees to give feedback on guest service policies.

- **The Power of Affinity Groups at Hyatt**: Hyatt's **Business Resource Groups (BRGs)**, like **Hyatt Mosaic**, provide a platform for employees to connect and share their experiences. These groups serve not only as support networks but also as critical drivers of innovation and inclusion within the company.

By sharing these narratives, the hospitality and tourism industry can better understand the lived experiences of diverse employees and guests, thereby identifying pathways to improve both internal culture and guest services.

Conclusion: The Need for Intentionality in Addressing Diversity

The state of diversity in today's hospitality and tourism industry reveals both progress and gaps that need to be addressed. While there are promising examples of hotels, CVBs, DMOs, and event venues working to improve diversity, equity, and inclusion, **there is still much work to be done**—particularly in creating more pathways for leadership roles and ensuring that diverse perspectives are represented at all levels of decision-making. When people of color are at the decision-making table and being solicited for their thoughts on how the company can do better, those suggestions are implemented, change for the better happens.

The key takeaway is that diversity is not just about ticking boxes or meeting quotas—it's about intentionality. It's about recognizing that different perspectives enrich the industry, making it more innovative, adaptable, and capable of serving a broader range of guests.

As we continue through this book, I hope to provide ways to move beyond numbers and quotas to create actionable strategies for fostering diversity, equity, and inclusion that truly makes a difference. It is only through these efforts that the industry can begin to close the gaps and build a future where all voices are heard, valued, and celebrated.

Hotels, CVBs, DMOs, Etc. can make remarkable strides from a profitability standpoint, if every fabric of human resources are considered and voices are heard. As a Meeting Planner for 10+ years, I take notice from the moment I do a Site Inspection until post-event where I receive reports, data, and information **PRIOR TO** receiving the final bill. Since I have already agreed to pay the bill, there's no need to rush it to me before letting me know how profitable our group was to the city and hotel. Spend data is not something I should have to beg or ask for. *Hint! Hint!*

References:

1. **Castell Project Study (2021)** – *"Black Representation in Hospitality Leadership."*

2. **McKinsey & Company Study (2020)** – *"Diversity Wins: How Inclusion Matters."*

3. **Marriott International's Diversity Efforts** – Global Diversity and Inclusion Council, Emerging Leaders Program.

4. **Hilton's Diversity & Inclusion Initiatives** – Team Member Resource Groups (TMRGs), leadership programs.

5. **IHG's IHG Academy and ERGs** – Community training programs, diversity in leadership, guest services.

CHAPTER 4

THE BUSINESS ADVANTAGE OF DIVERSITY, EQUITY, AND INCLUSION

Diversity, equity, and inclusion are often viewed as social imperatives—ethical necessities for creating fairness and equality in society. However, **they are also powerful business drivers**. In the hospitality and tourism industry, embracing diversity, equity, and inclusion has been shown to improve creativity, decision-making, and customer satisfaction, all of which directly contribute to a company's bottom line. This chapter explores how businesses in this industry can leverage the power of diversity, equity, and inclusion to unlock new markets, enhance guest experiences, and drive profitable growth.

Why Diversity and Inclusion Matter in Business

Diversity in the workplace means employing a mix of individuals with different backgrounds, experiences, and perspectives; *Equity* refers to creating fair opportunities and removing barriers so that everyone, regardless of their background, can thrive; while *Inclusion* ensures that these diverse voices are heard, valued, and actively involved in decision-making. In the hospitality and tourism industry, this means not only hiring a workforce that reflects the guests they serve but also empowering that workforce to inform policies, services, and strategies. Working together as a team has a way of bringing the goals of the company to life.

The business advantages of diversity, equity, and inclusion are well-documented across industries, and they hold particularly true in hospitality and tourism. Diverse and inclusive teams are better equipped to understand the needs and preferences of a wide range of customers. **When leadership teams reflect their diverse clientele, they are more likely to anticipate market demands, innovate effectively, and provide services that resonate with a variety of cultural backgrounds.**

The Connection Between Diversity and Innovation

One of the clearest benefits of diversity is its impact on innovation. The hospitality and tourism industry thrives on creativity and new ideas—whether it's designing unique guest experiences, crafting memorable marketing campaigns, or developing new service offerings. When teams are composed of people from diverse backgrounds, they bring different ways of thinking, unique insights, and varied approaches to problem-solving. This diversity of thought fosters a culture of innovation and helps businesses differentiate themselves in a competitive market.

Case Study: Airbnb's "Belong Anywhere" Campaign

Airbnb, the global home-sharing platform, provides a compelling example of how diversity can drive innovation. In 2016, the company launched its **Belong Anywhere** campaign, which focused on making every guest feel welcome, regardless of their background. The campaign emerged partly in response to reports of discrimination by Airbnb hosts and aimed to emphasize inclusivity as a core company value. This effort was informed by a diverse team that understood the significance of cultural sensitivity and the importance of belonging in travel experiences.

As a result, the campaign not only improved Airbnb's brand image but also expanded its market reach. By showcasing a commitment to diversity, equity, and inclusion, Airbnb attracted a broader customer base, including travelers from underrepresented groups who felt more comfortable using the platform. The success of the **Belong Anywhere** campaign is a testament to how diverse perspectives can shape business strategies that resonate with global audiences.

Diverse Perspectives, Better Decision-Making

Diverse teams make better decisions because they approach problems from multiple angles. This is particularly important in the hospitality and tourism industry, where understanding guest preferences, anticipating market trends, and responding to cultural sensitivities are crucial for success. Research from **Harvard Business Review** has shown that teams with greater diversity are more likely to reconsider facts, debate ideas more robustly, and make more accurate decisions, all of which contribute to improved business performance.

Marriott's Global Diversity Council:

Marriott International's **Global Diversity and Inclusion Council** serves as a strong example of how diverse leadership enhances decision-making. By bringing together leaders from different cultural, gender, sexual orientation, socioeconomic, and experiential backgrounds, the council provides guidance on policies, talent development, and marketing strategies to ensure that Marriott's services are inclusive and responsive to diverse guest needs. This approach has led to tangible business benefits, including higher guest satisfaction scores and increased market share in key demographics.

Capturing Untapped Markets through Inclusion

Diversity, Equity, and Inclusion open doors to untapped markets. The hospitality and tourism industry caters to a wide variety of travelers, from solo backpackers and family vacationers to business travelers and cultural tourists. By adopting an inclusive approach, businesses can connect with markets that may have been previously overlooked or underserved.

For example, the LGBTQ+ travel market is a growing segment with significant economic potential. According to the **International LGBTQ+ Travel Association (IGLTA)**, LGBTQ+ travelers contribute an estimated **$211 billion annually** to the global travel economy. Hotels and tourism companies that actively market to and create welcoming environments for LGBTQ+ travelers can tap into this lucrative market.

Hilton's Hilton Pride Initiative:

Hilton has actively pursued this market through its **Hilton Pride** initiative, which aims to create inclusive experiences for LGBTQ+ guests. The company has implemented inclusive marketing campaigns, trained staff on LGBTQ+ cultural sensitivity, and supported LGBTQ+ community events. This approach has helped Hilton build brand loyalty within the LGBTQ+ community and positioned the company as a welcoming choice for diverse travelers.

Enhancing the Guest Experience through Cultural Competence

Cultural competence is closely tied to guest satisfaction. When hospitality and tourism businesses demonstrate an understanding of different cultural preferences, traditions, and needs, guests feel valued and respected. This, in turn, enhances the overall guest experience and builds brand loyalty.

DoubleTree by Hilton's Global Service Adaptations:

DoubleTree by Hilton's approach to cultural competence provides a strong example of how to enhance guest experiences. By localizing services to meet the needs of diverse guests, DoubleTree adapts its hospitality offerings in different regions. For instance, properties in Asia may offer preferred bedding types and local breakfast options, while those in the Middle East provide Halal food, prayer spaces, and accommodations for religious observances. These adaptations demonstrate a commitment to understanding and respecting guests' cultural needs, resulting in positive guest feedback and stronger brand affinity.

IHG's Inclusive Marketing and Guest Services:

IHG's strategy of tailoring guest services to reflect local cultures also speaks to the importance of cultural competence. Whether offering language support for international travelers, creating menus that reflect regional preferences, or designing marketing campaigns that celebrate different cultural holidays, IHG's inclusive approach has contributed to positive guest experiences and brand recognition in global markets.

Financial Benefits of Embracing Diversity and Inclusion

There is a growing body of evidence linking diversity, equity, and inclusion to financial performance. A **Deloitte study** found that inclusive companies are **1.8 times more likely** to be change-ready and **1.7 times more likely** to be innovation leaders in their market. Furthermore, **McKinsey & Company's 2020 study** showed that companies in the top quartile for ethnic and cultural diversity were **36% more likely** to outperform their peers financially.

These findings make a compelling business case for hospitality and tourism companies to invest in diversity, equity, and inclusion as part of their overall strategy. By fostering diverse teams, giving equity in decision making practices, and creating inclusive environments; businesses can improve their service offerings, strengthen their brand, and ultimately drive greater profitability.

Conclusion: Diversity as a Business Imperative

The hospitality and tourism industry has much to gain from embracing diversity, equity, and inclusion. Not only do these values align with the fundamental principles of hospitality—welcoming and serving all people—but they also provide clear business advantages. Diverse and inclusive teams lead to better decision-making, more innovative solutions, and stronger connections with a broader customer base.

Moreover, the financial benefits of diversity, equity, and inclusion underscore the importance of integrating these principles into every aspect of business operations. From the front-line staff to the executive suite, fostering a culture of inclusion is not just a social responsibility—it is a business imperative that can enhance guest experiences, improve brand loyalty, and drive financial success.

As we move forward in this book, I will continue to explore how hospitality and tourism companies can implement best practices for inclusion, build culturally competent teams, and create a diverse future for the industry. The basic step is to have a self-reflective conversation to determine how diverse your leadership and management team is, then take action from there. Also, sharing equity in decision making & planning goes a long way in building trust within.

References:

1. **Airbnb's Belong Anywhere Campaign** – Case study on inclusive marketing and brand expansion.

2. **Harvard Business Review on Diversity and Decision-Making** – Research on the benefits of diverse teams.

3. **International LGBTQ+ Travel Association (IGLTA)** – Economic impact of LGBTQ+ travelers.

4. **Deloitte and McKinsey & Company Studies** – Financial benefits of diversity and inclusion in business.

5. **Hilton Pride Initiative** – Hilton's approach to LGBTQ+ inclusivity.

6. **DoubleTree by Hilton's Global Service Adaptations** – Case study on cultural competence in hospitality.

7. **IHG's Inclusive Marketing and Guest Services** – Examples of culturally tailored guest experiences.

CHAPTER 5

CULTURAL COMPETENCE IN ACTION: BEST PRACTICIES AND STRATEGIES

Understanding cultural competence and the value of diversity, equity, and inclusion is one thing, but implementing these concepts effectively is another. For hospitality and tourism businesses to reap the full benefits of an inclusive approach, they must develop actionable strategies and best practices that permeate every level of the organization—from front-line staff to the executive boardroom. This chapter will delve into the practical steps companies can take to build cultural competence, create an inclusive environment, and improve their service offerings for diverse guests.

Building Cultural Competence: Training and Education

<u>**Training is the foundation of cultural competence**</u>. For hospitality and tourism businesses to truly serve a diverse

clientele, every team member—from the front desk to housekeeping to upper management—must be equipped with the knowledge and skills to understand and respect different cultures.

1. **Cultural Sensitivity Training:**

The first step in fostering cultural competence is to provide comprehensive training on cultural sensitivity. This training helps staff understand the nuances of different cultures, learn how to interact respectfully, and become aware of common biases and stereotypes. For example, a training session may cover proper ways to greet guests from different regions, dietary customs and restrictions (*such as Halal or Kosher*), and how to respond to specific cultural or religious requests.

Case Study: Hyatt's Cultural Training Program

Hyatt's global cultural training program serves as a strong example of how to build cultural competence through education. Hyatt offers tailored training sessions for employees at every level, emphasizing the importance of understanding diverse cultures and traditions. One training module focuses on understanding Asian travelers, covering topics like dining preferences, language etiquette, and customs around hospitality. This has helped Hyatt's staff provide a warm and personalized experience for Asian guests and has contributed to positive feedback and increased brand loyalty in Asian markets.

Creating a Culturally Competent Workplace Culture

Building cultural competence requires more than just training—it also means creating a workplace culture where diversity is celebrated, equity is shared, inclusion is practiced, and every team member feels valued.

2. <u>Establishing Employee Resource Groups (ERGs) or Business Resource Groups (BRGs):</u>

ERGs and BRGs offer a platform for employees to connect with others who share similar cultural backgrounds or experiences. These groups not only provide support networks but also contribute to the organization's cultural competence by offering insights and recommendations on improving guest services, creating inclusive policies, and marketing to diverse communities.

Case Study: Hilton's Team Member Resource Groups (TMRGs)

Hilton's TMRGs are a powerful tool for promoting cultural competence within the company. Each group is formed around a specific demographic or interest, such as **Hilton Pride** for LGBTQ+ employees or **Abilities in Motion** for employees with disabilities. These TMRGs provide feedback on company policies, help shape inclusive marketing strategies and offer a safe space for employees to share their experiences. This has strengthened Hilton's internal culture and led to more inclusive guest experiences.

3. **Encouraging Open Dialogue and Feedback:**

Encouraging open dialogue about diversity and cultural competence is critical to building an inclusive workplace culture. Employees should feel comfortable sharing their perspectives, asking questions, and offering suggestions for improvement. This creates an environment where continuous learning and growth are valued, and where team members can collectively contribute to enhancing the guest experience.

Tailoring Services to Meet Cultural Needs

Cultural competence extends to the services that hospitality and tourism businesses provide to their guests. By tailoring services to reflect the needs and preferences of diverse clientele, companies can create memorable experiences that resonate with their guests.

4. **Adapting Food and Beverage Options:**

One of the most significant aspects of cultural competence in hospitality is **food**. Since dietary customs and preferences vary widely across cultures, offering a variety of menu options that cater to different needs is essential. Hotels and event venues should provide Halal, Kosher, Vegetarian,

Vegan, Gluten-free, and Allergen-friendly options, and ensure that their staff is trained to understand and respect these dietary needs.

DoubleTree by Hilton's Culinary Inclusivity

DoubleTree by Hilton's attention to dietary inclusivity is a prime example of how hospitality and tourism businesses can enhance cultural competence. At DoubleTree properties around the world, menus are designed to reflect local flavors while offering options that meet diverse dietary needs. In Middle Eastern markets, Halal food is standard, while in properties in Southeast Asia, dishes reflect local vegetarian traditions. This approach not only accommodates diverse guests but also introduces them to local culinary experiences in a culturally sensitive way.

5. Language and Communication Support:

Providing language support is an important aspect of cultural competence. Offering multilingual services, whether through bilingual staff, translated materials, or digital tools like mobile apps, helps guests feel more comfortable and ensures that their needs are met. It also demonstrates respect for their culture and can enhance the overall guest experience.

Case Study: IHG's Multilingual Services

IHG (**InterContinental Hotels Group**) demonstrates cultural competence through its commitment to providing language support to international guests. Many of IHG's properties employ multilingual staff who can assist guests in their native languages, while hotels like **InterContinental Hotels & Resorts** offer translated menus, guest information booklets, and digital tools to assist travelers. This focus on communication has enhanced guest experiences for non-English-speaking travelers and strengthened IHG's reputation for inclusivity.

Empowering Leadership and Diversity in Decision-Making

Cultural competence requires buy-in from leadership. It's important that decision-makers are not only diverse themselves but also understand the value of diversity, equity, and inclusion. Empowering leaders to take action on cultural competence is crucial for driving change throughout the organization.

6. <u>Creating a Diverse Leadership Pipeline:</u>

Building a diverse leadership team is essential for reflecting the company's customer base and fostering inclusive decision-making. Initiatives like mentorship programs, leadership training, and targeted recruitment can help elevate diverse talent to senior positions, ensuring that a variety of perspectives are represented at the top levels of the organization.

Marriott's Emerging Leaders Program

Marriott International's **Emerging Leaders Program** is designed to build a diverse leadership pipeline by providing mentorship, development, and career advancement opportunities for women and people of color. Through this program, Marriott aims to ensure that its leadership team reflects the diversity of its workforce and customer base, enabling the company to make more informed and inclusive decisions.

7. <u>Measuring Progress and Accountability:</u>

To ensure that cultural competence initiatives are effective, hospitality and tourism businesses must establish measurable goals and track their progress. This might include setting targets for diverse hiring, tracking guest satisfaction scores across different demographics, and evaluating the success of inclusive marketing campaigns. **Holding leadership accountable** for achieving these goals is key to creating lasting change.

Hilton's Diversity and Inclusion Dashboard

Hilton uses a **Diversity and Inclusion Dashboard** to measure the impact of its initiatives across the company. The dashboard tracks metrics like diverse hiring rates, employee satisfaction, and supplier diversity, allowing the company to identify areas of improvement and celebrate successes. This data-driven approach provides transparency and ensures that Hilton remains committed to its diversity and cultural competence goals.

Engaging with Diverse Communities and Partnerships

An effective way to build cultural competence is to **engage directly with the communities your business serves**. By forming partnerships with community organizations, advocacy groups, and cultural associations, hospitality and tourism companies can gain insights into the needs and preferences of their diverse clientele.

8. **Community Engagement and Partnerships:**

Working with diverse community organizations allows businesses to build trust and connections, making them more culturally competent and attuned to the needs of specific demographics. These partnerships can also lead to business opportunities, such as hosting culturally significant events, sponsoring local festivals, or offering services tailored to the community's needs.

IHG's Community-Centric Approach with IHG Academy

Through **IHG Academy**, IHG partners with educational institutions and community organizations to provide skills training and employment opportunities to young people, women, and underrepresented communities. By engaging with these communities directly, IHG builds cultural competence and strengthens its workforce with team members who reflect diverse cultures and bring unique perspectives to guest services.

Conclusion: Best Practices for a Culturally Competent Industry

Developing cultural competence is an ongoing journey that requires dedication, education, and a willingness to learn and adapt. By implementing best practices such as cultural sensitivity training, establishing employee resource groups, tailoring services to diverse needs, building a diverse leadership pipeline, and engaging with local communities, hospitality and tourism companies can create more inclusive environments for their employees and guests alike.

These strategies are not just good practices—they are essential to thriving in a global industry where *every guest's experience matters*. As we continue to explore the roadmap to a more diverse and inclusive future in hospitality and tourism, these best practices will serve as the building blocks for sustainable success and meaningful impact.

References:

1. **Hyatt's Cultural Training Program** – Hyatt's global training efforts for diverse guest service.

2. **Hilton's Team Member Resource Groups (TMRGs)** – Groups fostering inclusion within Hilton.

3. **DoubleTree by Hilton's Culinary Inclusivity** – Dietary-inclusive menu design for diverse guests.

4. **IHG's Multilingual Services** – IHG's commitment to providing language support.

5. **Marriott's Emerging Leaders Program** – Program to elevate diverse talent to leadership roles.

6. **Hilton's Diversity and Inclusion Dashboard** – Tool for measuring diversity initiatives.

7. **IHG Academy's Community Engagement** – IHG's program to provide training and employment opportunities.

CHAPTER 6

CREATING A DIVERSE FUTURE FOR THE HOSPITALITY & TOURISM INDUSTRY

The hospitality and tourism industry has always been shaped by the people it serves—diverse travelers seeking experiences that reflect their interests, cultures, and values. As our country and the world becomes increasingly interconnected and multicultural, it is more crucial than ever for the industry to move beyond token representation and build a future where diversity and cultural competence are the standards, not exceptions. This chapter will outline a vision for what this diverse future could look like, discuss the opportunities it presents, and provide actionable steps that Hotels, CVBs, DMOs, and event venues can take to create a more inclusive and culturally competent industry.

The Vision of a Truly Diverse and Inclusive Industry

A diverse future in hospitality and tourism means building an industry where all voices are heard, all identities are respected, and all guests feel welcomed. This vision is grounded in three key principles: **representation, inclusivity, and equity.**

Representation means that leadership teams, front-line staff, and decision-makers reflect the diversity of the communities and guests they serve. **Inclusivity** means creating environments where everyone, regardless of their background or identity, can fully participate, contribute, and feel valued. **Equity** ensures that policies, practices, and opportunities are designed to support those who have been historically marginalized, addressing barriers to access and advancement.

Achieving this vision requires the industry to adopt a mindset of continuous improvement and cultural humility— a commitment to learning from diverse perspectives, adapting to changing needs, and striving to make hospitality and tourism experiences equitable for all.

Opportunities of Embracing a Diverse Future

The benefits of building a diverse and inclusive future are multifaceted and extend beyond social responsibility. Here are some key opportunities that this vision provides:

1. **Connecting with Emerging Markets and Traveler Demographics**: The world's travel demographics are changing rapidly. According to the **World Tourism Organization (UNWTO)**, international travel is becoming more diverse, with increasing numbers of travelers from Africa, Asia, Latin America, and the Middle East. There is also a growing segment of travelers who identify as LGBTQ+, are multigenerational, or come from multicultural backgrounds. By embracing diversity, equity, and inclusivity, the industry can attract and connect with these emerging markets, enhancing their travel experiences and building brand loyalty.

2. **Enhancing the Guest Experience through Personalization**: Personalized service is a hallmark of the hospitality and tourism industry, and understanding cultural preferences is key to delivering exceptional guest experiences. Hotels that cater to cultural traditions—such as offering traditional breakfast options for Indian travelers, creating child-friendly spaces for Middle Eastern families, or providing language support for Chinese-speaking guests—show respect for their guests' identities and create memorable experiences.

3. **Promoting Inclusive Economic Development**: The hospitality and tourism industry play a vital role in local economies, providing jobs, supporting small

businesses, and contributing to community development. By actively working with diverse suppliers, hiring a multicultural workforce, and partnering with local cultural organizations, the industry can promote inclusive economic growth that benefits all communities, particularly those that have historically been marginalized.

Case Study: Hyatt's *"Change Starts Here"* Initiative

In 2021, **Hyatt Hotels Corporation** launched the **Change Starts Here** initiative to build a diverse and inclusive culture within the company. This multi-year effort focuses on increasing diverse representation at all levels of the organization, enhancing workplace inclusivity, and driving business results by integrating diversity, equity, and inclusion into its service model. As part of the initiative, Hyatt has set specific targets for increasing diverse talent in leadership roles, investing in diverse suppliers, and supporting programs that benefit underrepresented communities.

By setting clear goals and creating accountability around diversity, equity, and inclusion, Hyatt is working to shape a future where all guests and employees feel seen, valued, and celebrated.

Practical Steps to Build a Diverse and Inclusive Future

Building a diverse, equitable, and inclusive future for the hospitality and tourism industry requires strategic planning, collaboration, and intentional action. Below are some practical steps that organizations can take to move toward this vision:

1. **Establish Clear Goals and Accountability Structures**
   To create meaningful change, organizations must set clear goals for diversity, equity, and inclusion and hold leaders accountable for achieving them. These goals should address areas like hiring, supplier diversity, inclusive marketing, and community engagement. Establishing an accountability structure, such as a **Diversity, Equity, and Inclusion (DEI) Council** or **Diversity Scorecard**, ensures that progress is tracked and that leaders are responsible for driving change.

2. **Foster Diverse Leadership Pipelines and Opportunities for Advancement**

Promoting diversity in leadership is essential for creating an inclusive future. Hospitality and tourism businesses can foster diverse talent by offering mentorship programs, leadership training, and pathways for advancement to employees from underrepresented backgrounds. It is also important to implement policies that prevent discrimination and bias in hiring and promotions.

Case Study: Marriott's Women's Leadership Development Initiative

Marriott International has long been recognized for its commitment to promoting women in leadership roles. Through its **Women's Leadership Development Initiative**, Marriott provides mentorship, sponsorship, and professional development programs aimed at advancing women's careers. The initiative has led to a significant increase in women holding executive roles within the company, demonstrating the power of intentional efforts to create opportunities for underrepresented groups.

3. Prioritize Supplier Diversity and Local Partnerships

Supplier diversity is a key component of building a diverse industry. Organizations should actively seek partnerships with minority-owned, women-owned, LGBTQ+-owned, and other diverse suppliers who reflect the communities they serve. These partnerships not only enhance the authenticity of guest experiences but also contribute to local economic development and build stronger connections with diverse communities.

IHG's Supplier Diversity Program

IHG has established a robust supplier diversity program, seeking out partnerships with businesses owned by people of color, women, and other underrepresented groups. By working closely with diverse suppliers to meet procurement needs across its properties, IHG supports inclusive economic growth and ensures that its services align with its guests' diverse cultural and business expectations.

4. Design Events and Experiences with Inclusivity in Mind

Event planning in hospitality and tourism requires a deep understanding of guests' cultural needs and preferences. For conventions, weddings, festivals, and corporate events, it's important to consider how everything from venue layout and accessibility to catering and entertainment reflects an inclusive and welcoming environment. Engaging diverse voices in the event planning process ensures that all attendees feel represented and respected.

Case Study: The Inclusive Redesign of a National Convention

A national convention held in the Midwest wanted to ensure that its annual event was more inclusive for its diverse members, including those from Black, Latinx, Asian, LGBTQ+, and disabled communities. The event organizers worked with a diversity consulting firm to redesign key aspects of the event, such as creating accessible registration and seating areas, providing gender-neutral restrooms, and offering culturally relevant entertainment. The result was an event that drew record attendance and garnered positive feedback for its inclusivity and cultural sensitivity.

5. **Engage in Community Outreach and Cultural Education**

To build cultural competence and foster stronger community connections, hospitality and tourism businesses should engage in outreach activities that promote diversity, equity, and inclusion. This can include hosting cultural events, sponsoring community festivals, supporting local nonprofits, and providing educational opportunities for employees to learn about different cultures and communities.

Hilton's Travel with Purpose Initiative

Through its **Travel with Purpose** initiative, Hilton demonstrates its commitment to diversity, inclusion, and community engagement. The initiative includes efforts to create positive social impact by supporting local communities, promoting cultural education, and encouraging volunteerism among team members. By aligning its corporate values with community needs, Hilton fosters a sense of belonging and inclusivity that extends to guests, employees, and community partners alike.

The Power of Collaboration: Working Together for a Diverse Industry

Creating a diverse future for the hospitality and tourism industry is a collective effort that requires collaboration between multiple stakeholders—hotels, CVBs, DMOs, event venues, travel companies, local governments, and community organizations. By working together, these stakeholders can share best practices, advocate for inclusive policies, and build partnerships that support a more equitable and diverse industry.

Partnership Example: American Hotel & Lodging Association (AHLA) and Diversity Initiatives

The **American Hotel & Lodging Association (AHLA)** has been a key partner in advancing diversity within the hospitality and tourism industry. Through its diversity initiatives, AHLA works with member hotels, policy makers, and advocacy groups to develop inclusive workplace policies, promote diverse hiring practices, and create pathways for leadership for women and people of color. AHLA's commitment to collaboration demonstrates the power of bringing industry players together to drive meaningful change.

Conclusion: Charting a Path Toward a Diverse and Inclusive Future

Building a diverse future for the hospitality and tourism industry requires more than just good intentions—it requires action, commitment, and accountability. By setting clear goals, fostering diverse leadership, designing inclusive events, supporting supplier diversity, and engaging with local communities, the industry can move toward a future where all guests are welcomed, all voices are heard, and all experiences are valued.

As the industry continues to evolve, businesses that embrace diversity, equity, and inclusion as **core principles** will not only create better guest experiences but also drive innovation, promote economic growth, and strengthen their communities. The path forward is clear, and the opportunities for a more inclusive and culturally competent industry are limitless. All we have to do is take the blinders off and see that the world of hospitality and tourism is changing around us and the demands of keeping up requires more people from those communities at the decision-making table. Business Resource Groups and Employee Resource Groups are great places to start.

References:

1. **UNWTO Reports on Global Travel Demographics** – Insights into emerging markets and travel patterns.

2. **Hyatt's Change Starts Here Initiative** – A multi-year effort to build a more inclusive culture.

3. **Marriott's Women's Leadership Development Initiative** – Programs for advancing women in leadership.

4. **IHG's Supplier Diversity Program** – Strategies for working with diverse suppliers.

5. **Hilton's Travel with Purpose Initiative** – Community engagement and cultural education.

6. **AHLA's Diversity Initiatives** – Collaborative efforts to promote diversity in hospitality.

CHAPTER 7

BUILDING PARTNERSHIPS FOR A DIVERSE INDUSTRY

The path to creating a diverse and inclusive hospitality and tourism industry is not one that any single company can walk alone. Building a truly inclusive industry requires collaboration and partnership among various stakeholders—hotels, CVBs, DMOs, event venues, travel associations, community organizations, advocacy groups, and even local governments. By developing partnerships that prioritize diversity and cultural competence, hospitality and tourism businesses can broaden their reach, enhance guest experiences, and make a meaningful impact on the communities they serve. This chapter will explore the power of partnerships in promoting diversity, equity, and inclusion and provide case studies and strategies for building successful collaborations.

Why Partnerships Matter in Diversity and Inclusion

The hospitality and tourism industry is a network of interconnected businesses and communities, no hotel or city is an island unto themselves where they don't need partnerships to be successful or profitable. A successful event, conference, convention, or destination experience is the result of various elements working in harmony—lodging, catering, transportation, entertainment, cultural programming, and more. Therefore, building a diverse and inclusive industry requires partnerships that ensure every aspect of the guest experience reflects cultural awareness, representation, and respect.

1. Leveraging Local Expertise and Cultural Knowledge

Partnering with local cultural organizations, minority business associations, and community groups allows hospitality and tourism businesses to gain insights into the cultural preferences, traditions, and expectations of the communities they serve. These partnerships are invaluable for understanding how to cater to diverse travelers and create authentic experiences that honor local cultures.

2. Expanding Market Reach through Advocacy Groups and Networks

Partnering with advocacy groups, such as organizations serving Black and Brown travelers, LGBTQ+ communities, or individuals with disabilities, provides access to networks and markets that may have been previously overlooked. These groups not only provide insights into the needs and preferences of specific communities but also help promote hotels, CVBs, DMOs, and venues as welcoming and inclusive spaces.

3. Supporting Community Development and Economic Empowerment

By working with local vendors, minority-owned businesses, and community initiatives, hospitality and tourism businesses can contribute to the economic development of the areas they operate in. These partnerships not only promote supplier diversity but also empower local entrepreneurs, contribute to job creation, and strengthen community ties.

Case Study: Collaborative Event Planning with Cultural Organizations

A large hotel in Washington, D.C., sought to enhance its cultural competence by building partnerships with local community organizations representing diverse cultures. The goal was to make the hotel a preferred venue for multicultural events, conferences, and celebrations, while also providing more inclusive guest experiences.

1. Partnership with Local Cultural Centers and Chambers of Commerce

The hotel formed partnerships with local cultural centers representing African American, Hispanic, Asian, and Middle Eastern communities. It also connected with Chambers of Commerce for minority-owned businesses, establishing itself as a preferred venue for culturally significant events such as Black History Month Celebrations, Asian American Business Conferences, Hispanic Heritage events, LGBTQ Pride Festivities, Etc.

These partnerships provided the hotel with access to a broad network of event organizers, vendors, and performers, enabling it to host events that authentically reflected the cultures of the communities it served. For example, the hotel worked with local African American chefs to curate menus for a Juneteenth celebration and partnered with Asian American performers to provide entertainment for a cultural festival.

2. Benefits and Impact

The hotel's commitment to building culturally relevant partnerships led to a steady increase in event bookings from diverse organizations, strengthened its reputation as an inclusive venue, and boosted community engagement. Additionally, by working with minority-owned vendors, the hotel contributed to the economic empowerment of local businesses.

Engaging Diverse Supplier Networks

One of the most impactful ways to promote diversity in hospitality and tourism is by developing partnerships with diverse suppliers. These partnerships enhance the authenticity of services and help build economic opportunities for underrepresented entrepreneurs.

Case Study: Hilton's Supplier Diversity Program

Hilton's supplier diversity program emphasizes building relationships with minority-owned, women-owned, LGBTQ+-owned, and veteran-owned businesses. The company's approach to developing diverse supplier networks involves more than just procurement—*it includes fostering long-term partnerships and providing support for business growth.*

1. Creating Supplier Opportunities and Training

Hilton works with various supplier diversity organizations, such as the **National Minority Supplier Development Council (NMSDC)**, to identify diverse vendors who meet the company's standards for quality, sustainability, and service. Once identified, Hilton provides these vendors with opportunities to engage with its procurement teams and participate in training programs designed to help small businesses navigate the hospitality and tourism industry.

2. Results and Community Impact

The emphasis on diverse supplier partnerships has led to a more culturally diverse supply chain and helped Hilton offer services that reflect the needs and preferences of its diverse guest base. The program also supports local communities by providing minority-owned businesses with access to larger markets and opportunities for growth.

Collaborations with Industry Associations and Advocacy Groups

Industry associations and advocacy groups play a key role in driving diversity, equity, and inclusion within hospitality and tourism. Collaborating with these organizations can provide access to resources, training, and best practices for creating an inclusive industry.

Case Study: IHG's Collaboration with the International LGBTQ+ Travel Association (IGLTA)

As part of its commitment to inclusivity, **InterContinental Hotels Group (IHG)** formed a strategic partnership with the **International LGBTQ+ Travel Association (IGLTA)**. IGLTA is a global network dedicated to advancing LGBTQ+ travel, promoting inclusivity, and providing resources for businesses to create safe and welcoming spaces for LGBTQ+ travelers.

1. **Training and Education on LGBTQ+ Cultural Competence**

Through its partnership with IGLTA, IHG provides training and educational resources to its hotel staff on LGBTQ+ cultural competence, including how to respect guests' pronouns, avoid assumptions about relationships, and provide an environment where LGBTQ+ guests feel safe and welcome. The collaboration also extends to marketing strategies that authentically represent LGBTQ+ travelers and events that celebrate LGBTQ+ culture.

2. **Business Benefits and Increased Guest Loyalty**

The partnership with IGLTA has enhanced IHG's ability to connect with LGBTQ+ travelers worldwide, resulting in positive guest feedback and increased loyalty within the LGBTQ+ community. By creating a welcoming environment and engaging with LGBTQ+ advocacy groups, IHG has strengthened its brand reputation as a leader in diversity, equity, and inclusion.

The Power of Community Engagement and Corporate Social Responsibility

Community engagement is a cornerstone of promoting diversity, equity, and inclusion. By supporting local cultural events, festivals, and social initiatives, hospitality and tourism businesses can strengthen their connection to the communities they serve and create a positive social impact.

Engaging communities means to become a part of their ecosystem and taking note of the things that are important to them and their community.

Intention must be reflected in actions. If you are interested in bringing in more business from communities of color, LGBTQ+ individuals, individuals with mobility challenges, etc.; seek out their local events and activities that your hotel, CVB, DMO, or venue can host and partner with them to host certain elements of their programming, if not all.

Case Study: Marriott's *"Spirit to Serve"* Community Engagement Program

Marriott International has a long-standing commitment to community engagement through its **Spirit to Serve** program. The initiative encourages Marriott employees to volunteer in their local communities, support diverse nonprofit organizations, and participate in cultural events.

1. Supporting Diverse Communities through Philanthropy and Volunteerism

The Spirit to Serve program includes philanthropic contributions to nonprofits serving diverse communities, as well as volunteer activities like supporting food banks, mentoring youth from underserved areas, and participating in cultural festivals. Marriott employees are also empowered to work with local organizations to address issues that matter to their communities, such as homelessness, education, and workforce development.

2. Impact on Community Relations and Brand Loyalty

By engaging in community service and supporting diverse causes, Marriott has built strong relationships with local communities and created a sense of shared purpose with its employees and guests. This approach to corporate social responsibility not only enhances the company's social impact but also contributes to increased brand loyalty among travelers who value socially responsible businesses.

Conclusion: Partnerships as a Catalyst for Diversity in Hospitality

The future of diversity, equity, and inclusion in the hospitality and tourism industry will be shaped by the partnerships that companies build with local communities, diverse suppliers, advocacy groups, and industry associations. By leveraging these partnerships, businesses can deepen their cultural competence, create authentic guest experiences, and drive economic empowerment in the communities they serve.

Partnerships are not just about transactional relationships; they are about building bridges, fostering understanding, and working together to create a more inclusive and welcoming industry for all. By prioritizing partnerships with a focus on diversity, equity, and inclusion; hospitality and tourism businesses can lead the way in creating a world where every traveler feels seen, valued, and embraced.

Have you considered partnering or working on a community service project with a nonprofit organization or business in your area? Afterwords, hold a brief and fun reception to thank all those who participated, and provide *"Certificates of Appreciation"* to those partners? A little bit goes a long way. Building social capital-based relationships can easily be converted into actual capital and revenue in the long run. *Something to think about!*

References:

1. **Hilton's Supplier Diversity Program** – Building diverse supply chains and supporting minority-owned businesses.

2. **IHG and IGLTA Partnership** – LGBTQ+ cultural competence training and inclusive marketing.

3. **Marriott's Spirit to Serve Program** – Community engagement and corporate social responsibility.

4. **Collaboration with Local Cultural Centers and Chambers of Commerce** – Enhancing event inclusivity through community partnerships.

5. **AHLA and Diversity Initiatives** – Working with industry associations to promote diversity in hospitality.

CHAPTER 8

BREAKING BARRIERS AND REDEFINING NARRATIVES

For far too long, the hospitality and tourism industry has operated with stereotypes, biases, and one-dimensional narratives that do not reflect the true diversity and richness of cultures, communities, and travelers. Breaking these barriers and redefining these narratives is crucial to creating an inclusive industry that respects, values, and serves people from all backgrounds. This chapter will explore how hospitality and tourism businesses can challenge stereotypes, address biases, and craft new narratives that reflect the complexity and beauty of the diverse communities they serve.

The Impact of Stereotypes and Biases in Hospitality

Stereotypes and biases in hospitality are often subtle yet pervasive. They can manifest in the form of marketing that lacks representation, service practices that fail to meet the needs of diverse guests, and assumptions about what certain groups of travelers want or need. These stereotypes can perpetuate exclusion, negatively impact the guest experience, and prevent businesses from effectively connecting with a broad range of customers.

1. Marketing Missteps and the "Single Story"

One of the most common ways stereotypes play out in hospitality and tourism is through marketing. Advertisements, brochures, and social media campaigns often reflect a narrow view of the *"ideal traveler,"* typically featuring affluent, white, able-bodied guests. This approach can alienate people of color, LGBTQ+ travelers, those with disabilities, and other groups who do not see themselves represented in hospitality and tourism branding.

The Power of Representation in Marketing To break these stereotypes, marketing materials should reflect the diversity of travelers by featuring people from different racial, ethnic, cultural, gender, sexual orientation, ability, and age backgrounds. For example, **Hilton's "Room for All" Campaign** showcased a variety of guests—from families of color to same-sex couples—enjoying stays at Hilton properties. By representing diverse guests in its advertising, Hilton effectively communicated that its properties were welcoming and inclusive to all travelers, helping to redefine the narrative of who belongs in hospitality and tourism.

2. Service Biases and Cultural Assumptions

Service bias often arises when staff members make assumptions based on stereotypes about what guests from certain backgrounds want or need. For example, assuming that all travelers from China will want tea in their rooms, or expecting that Muslim guests will not drink alcohol, can lead to awkward or uncomfortable interactions. While these assumptions are often well-meaning, they can also reduce guests to a single aspect of their identity and fail to consider their individual preferences.

Case Study: Inclusive Service at Marriott International

To address service bias, **Marriott International** implemented a training program called *"Serve with Pride,"* which focuses on providing inclusive service to guests from all cultural backgrounds. The training emphasizes listening to each guest's individual preferences, offering culturally relevant options without assumptions, and creating an environment where all guests feel respected and valued. The training has resulted in improved guest satisfaction scores, particularly among diverse traveler groups who appreciate being treated as individuals rather than stereotypes.

Challenging Stereotypes through Cultural Storytelling

Redefining narratives in hospitality and tourism requires actively sharing and amplifying the stories, histories, and experiences of underrepresented communities. Cultural storytelling is a powerful way to break down stereotypes, build empathy, and showcase the depth and diversity of cultures beyond one-dimensional representations.

1. Elevating Local Narratives and Community Voices

One approach to cultural storytelling is to highlight the stories and contributions of the communities in which hotels, CVBs, DMOs, and event venues operate. By collaborating with local artists, historians, and cultural leaders, businesses can create experiences that reflect the true character and history of the area.

Case Study: The Hotel Zena's Celebration of Female Empowerment

Hotel Zena in Washington, D.C. offers a strong example of elevating local narratives and challenging traditional hospitality and tourism stereotypes. The hotel, which describes itself as a *"feminist hotel,"* is designed to celebrate the achievements and contributions of women, with an emphasis on gender equality and empowerment. The hotel's art collection features portraits of influential women, local female artists, and interactive exhibits that tell stories of gender equity movements. This approach creates a powerful guest experience that challenges stereotypes and redefines the narrative of what hospitality and tourism can represent.

2. Incorporating Cultural Elements into Guest Experiences

In addition to visual storytelling, hospitality and tourism businesses can incorporate cultural elements into guest experiences through food, music, art, and entertainment. By offering guests the opportunity to learn about and engage with different cultures, businesses create authentic connections and foster cross-cultural understanding.

IHG's Global Local Program

InterContinental Hotels Group (IHG) has launched the **Global Local Program**, which allows guests to immerse themselves in the local culture of their destination. Through partnerships with local chefs, artists, and tour operators, IHG properties offer culturally themed experiences such as cooking classes featuring traditional dishes, art installations by local artists, and guided tours that showcase the heritage of the surrounding area. This program not only enhances the guest experience but also promotes cultural appreciation and breaks down stereotypes by allowing travelers to experience destinations from an authentic perspective.

Empowering Diverse Voices in Hospitality Leadership

Redefining narratives also requires empowering diverse voices within the hospitality and tourism industry itself. Representation in leadership is crucial for shaping the direction of businesses, policies, and guest services in ways that reflect a commitment to inclusion.

1. Creating Platforms for Underrepresented Voices

Organizations can create platforms for underrepresented voices to share their experiences, ideas, and perspectives. This may include mentorship programs for employees of color, forums for women leaders to discuss challenges and opportunities, or advisory councils for LGBTQ+ employees. Ensuring that diverse voices are heard and valued in decision-making processes allows for more equitable and inclusive business practices.

Case Study: Hilton's CEO Light & Warmth Award

Hilton's CEO Light & Warmth Award recognizes team members who go above and beyond to create an inclusive culture within the company. Past recipients of the award have included front-line staff who have advocated for inclusive policies, managers who have championed supplier diversity, and teams who have developed programs to support communities of color. By celebrating the achievements of employees who promote diversity, equity, and inclusion, Hilton not only empowers underrepresented voices but also reinforces the values of equity and respect throughout its organization.

2. Leadership Development and Sponsorship for Diverse Talent

Leadership development programs that specifically support diverse talent are essential for breaking barriers to advancement and redefining the narratives of who can lead in hospitality and tourism. Sponsorship—*where senior leaders actively advocate for the career advancement of diverse employees*—is particularly impactful for creating pathways to leadership roles.

Accor's RiiSE Network

Accor Hotels launched the **RiiSE Network**, a global program aimed at supporting gender equality and cultural diversity within the company's leadership. **RiiSE** focuses on mentorship, sponsorship, and development opportunities for women and employees from underrepresented backgrounds. The program's goal is to elevate diverse talent to senior positions within Accor's properties, ensuring that leadership teams reflect a commitment to diversity and inclusivity.

Crafting Authentic and Culturally Competent Marketing Strategies

Marketing plays a crucial role in redefining narratives and showcasing the values of diversity, equity, and inclusion. To craft authentic marketing strategies, hospitality and tourism businesses must go beyond surface-level representation and tell stories that resonate with the diverse communities they wish to serve.

1. Collaborating with Diverse Creatives and Influencers

One effective way to create culturally competent marketing is by collaborating with creatives and influencers who represent the communities being featured. These individuals bring their lived experiences and cultural insights to the storytelling process, ensuring that campaigns are genuine and respectful.

2. Avoiding Tokenism and Cultural Appropriation

It is important to avoid tokenism—using a single person or image to represent an entire culture—or cultural appropriation, which involves taking elements of a culture without permission or understanding. Marketing campaigns should be designed with input from the communities being represented and should aim to showcase the diversity within cultures, rather than reinforcing stereotypes.

Case Study: Airbnb's *"We Accept"* Campaign

Airbnb's *"We Accept"* campaign was a global initiative that highlighted the company's commitment to inclusivity and acceptance. The campaign featured diverse guests of different races, ages, abilities, and gender identities, along with stories of belonging and acceptance from around the world. Airbnb's approach to telling authentic stories and partnering with diverse influencers allowed the campaign to resonate with a broad range of travelers and reinforce the company's brand values.

Conclusion: Redefining the Hospitality Narrative for the Future

Redefining narratives in the hospitality and tourism industry is about more than just changing imagery or messaging—it's about challenging stereotypes, addressing biases, and creating inclusive environments where all guests and employees feel seen and valued. By breaking down barriers, sharing diverse stories, empowering underrepresented voices, and crafting authentic marketing strategies, hospitality and tourism businesses can shape a future that reflects the true diversity of the world we live in.

Imagery and representation are important though, a few things I look for when I go on FAM (*Familiarization*) Tours are: (1) how many Black or Brown people are in decision-making positions or are they just tokens along for the presentation; (2) pictures of Black and Brown people on the wall in primarily white establishments; (3) are there people of color in leadership and management positions in the places I am being shown or shopped around to; and (4) my personal preference requests prior to traveling (*from the airline to the amenities offered in the room*). If you truly want me to bring a convention, conference, or meeting to your property, city, venue – make sure I can see myself and the market of those I am bringing in your marketing materials, advertisements, and people.

As the industry continues to evolve, the opportunity to redefine narratives is not just a responsibility—it's a chance to build deeper connections, create richer experiences, and celebrate the diversity that makes travel so meaningful. The work to change perceptions, elevate diverse voices, and tell stories of inclusion is ongoing, but it is a journey worth taking, one story at a time. I believe the best of hospitality and tourism can only be realized when those in the C Suites reflect the diversity of those in the workforce. Also, when equity is given to the many voices that make up the industry and help to ensure all touchpoints that have direct and/or indirect financial benefits are at the table. They too deserve a seat at the decision-making table because they know the customers and guest BETTER than those at the top.

References:

1. **Hilton's "Room for All" Campaign** – Inclusive marketing and representation.

2. **Marriott's Serve with Pride Program** – Training on inclusive service practices.

3. **Hotel Zena's Feminist Design Concept** – Elevating local narratives through cultural storytelling.

4. **IHG's Global Local Program** – Culturally themed guest experiences and local partnerships.

5. **Hilton's CEO Light & Warmth Award** – Recognizing diversity and inclusion champions.

6. **Accor's RiiSE Network** – Leadership development for gender equality and cultural diversity.

7. **Airbnb's "We Accept" Campaign** – Authentic marketing with a focus on inclusivity.

CHAPTER 9

PREPARING FOR A GLOBAL MARKET: EMBRACING CULTURAL COMPETENCE IN A CHANGING WORLD

As the hospitality and tourism industry continues to evolve, there is a growing need to prepare for a global market—one where travelers come from increasingly diverse backgrounds and cultures, and where their needs, preferences, and expectations are shaped by complex social, economic, and political factors. Embracing cultural competence is no longer just an option; it is a requirement for businesses that wish to thrive in a world that is constantly changing and becoming more interconnected. In this chapter, we will dive deep into how the global market is shifting, explore the challenges and opportunities that come with serving a diverse international clientele, and I'll do my best to provide actionable steps for hospitality and tourism businesses to stay ahead in the game.

Understanding the Shifting Global Travel Landscape

The global travel market has undergone significant changes over the past decade, driven by rising middle classes in emerging markets, increased mobility, and the growth of technology that connects travelers with destinations around the world. Key trends that are reshaping the global travel landscape include:

1. **The Rise of Emerging Markets and Multicultural Travelers.** Travel is no longer dominated by traditional Western markets. According to the **World Travel & Tourism Council (WTTC)**, travel demand from emerging markets—particularly from China, India, Africa, Southeast Asia, and Latin America—has seen rapid growth. The **UNWTO** projects that by 2030, Asia-Pacific travelers will represent almost a third of the global tourism market, while travel from Africa and Latin America will continue to increase steadily. This trend is redefining what the global traveler looks like and brings unique cultural preferences to the forefront of hospitality and tourism.

For example, Chinese travelers—the world's largest outbound travel market—bring specific expectations around service, language support, and dining experiences. Indian travelers often travel with extended families, seeking accommodations that cater to multigenerational groups. African travelers, with their diverse nations and cultures, bring unique culinary, music, and entertainment preferences that reflect their regional identities. Latin American travelers value warm, friendly service and are often looking for immersive experiences that connect them to local culture.

2. **The Increasing Demand for Authentic and Experiential Travel.** Today's travelers are seeking more than just sightseeing; they are looking for experiences that allow them to connect with local cultures, explore new ways of life, and participate in authentic activities. This has given rise to *"experiential travel,"* where guests prioritize engaging with the destination's food, art, history, and people. As a result, hospitality and tourism businesses must go beyond traditional service offerings and create experiences that allow guests to immerse themselves in the culture of the places they visit.

Case Study: Marriott's Bonvoy Moments

Marriott International's Bonvoy Moments initiative is an example of how hospitality and tourism businesses can tap into experiential travel. Through Bonvoy Moments, members of the Marriott Bonvoy loyalty program can bid on or purchase exclusive experiences that are tied to local culture, such as cooking classes with renowned chefs, music concerts, adventure sports, and guided tours that offer insider access to unique places. By curating culturally rich experiences, Marriott enhances its guest loyalty and positions itself as a brand that understands and caters to the desires of the modern traveler.

3. **Emphasis on Wellness, Safety, and Sustainability**
   The modern traveler is increasingly concerned about personal wellness, safety, and environmental sustainability. The **COVID-19 pandemic** heightened these concerns, leading travelers to prioritize cleanliness, health protocols, and physical safety. Additionally, there is a growing demand for sustainable travel practices, as environmentally conscious travelers seek out hotels and experiences that minimize their carbon footprint, support local communities, and promote responsible tourism.

IHG's Green Engage Program

InterContinental Hotels Group (IHG) launched the **Green Engage Program**, which helps its properties minimize their environmental impact through energy efficiency, water conservation, and waste reduction initiatives. The program not only addresses the growing demand for sustainability but also demonstrates IHG's commitment to being a responsible brand that supports environmental well-being.

Challenges and Opportunities in Serving a Diverse Global Clientele

Serving a global clientele comes with both challenges and opportunities. Cultural differences, language barriers, and varying traveler preferences can make it difficult for hospitality and tourism businesses to deliver seamless and personalized service. However, those who embrace these challenges have the opportunity to stand out and gain a competitive edge by offering experiences that resonate deeply with guests.

1. Cultural Competence and Personalization in Guest Services

One of the primary challenges in serving global travelers is understanding their diverse cultural preferences and finding ways to provide personalized service that meets their needs. This requires not only awareness of different cultural customs but also the flexibility to adapt services accordingly. For example:

- **Language Support and Multilingual Services**: Providing multilingual services, such as bilingual staff, translated materials, and digital language support, helps bridge communication gaps and ensures that guests feel comfortable and understood. According to a study by **Expedia Group**, travelers from non-English speaking countries are more likely to book with hotels that offer services in their native language.

- **Respect for Religious and Dietary Preferences**: A key component of cultural competence is understanding religious practices and dietary restrictions. Hotels and venues should ensure that they offer food options that cater to Halal, Kosher, Vegetarian, Vegan, and Allergen-Friendly diets, and that they respect guests' religious observances, such as offering prayer spaces or making accommodations for fasting during religious periods like Ramadan.

Case Study: Accor Hotels and Cultural Adaptation

Accor Hotels has implemented cultural adaptation across its properties to cater to the needs of global travelers. In properties in the Middle East, Accor provides Halal-certified food, gender-segregated swimming pools, and prayer rooms to meet the needs of Muslim guests. In Asian properties, breakfast menus include a variety of Asian dishes, and staff are trained to greet guests in local languages. This commitment to cultural adaptation helps Accor properties create a sense of belonging for guests and enhance their overall experience.

2. **Digital Transformation and Guest Experience Enhancement**

Technology plays a crucial role in enhancing the guest experience for a global clientele. Digital tools such as mobile apps, chatbots, online concierge services, and contactless payment systems not only improve convenience but also help overcome language barriers and provide personalized recommendations based on guests' preferences.

Hilton Honors App and Digital Key

Hilton's Honors App allows guests to check in, choose their rooms, access hotel amenities, and even use their smartphones as digital room keys. By offering a contactless and personalized experience, the app provides global travelers with a sense of convenience and safety, particularly in the post-pandemic world. The app also supports multiple languages, ensuring that international guests can navigate the app with ease.

Building Global Partnerships for Cultural Competence

To prepare for a global market, hospitality and tourism businesses need to build partnerships that enhance their cultural competence, extend their reach to diverse traveler groups, and provide guests with authentic and immersive experiences.

1. Partnering with Local Cultural Experts and Tour Operators

One of the most effective ways to enhance cultural competence is to partner with local experts, tour operators, and cultural organizations. These partnerships provide businesses with insights into the local culture, traditions, and expectations of guests from diverse backgrounds. For example, hotels can collaborate with local chefs to offer cooking classes, work with cultural centers to organize art exhibits, or partner with tour guides to offer heritage tours that showcase the destination's unique history.

Case Study: Hyatt's *"Find"* Experiences

Hyatt Hotels Corporation introduced **Find Experiences**, a collection of curated activities that allow guests to explore the local culture of their destination. From food tours to wellness workshops, these experiences are designed in partnership with local experts and artisans to ensure authenticity. By offering guests culturally immersive experiences that connect them to the local community, Hyatt strengthens its appeal to global travelers who seek meaningful and memorable stays.

2. Engaging with Global Travel Associations and Advocacy Groups

Global travel associations, such as the **World Travel & Tourism Council (WTTC)**, **International LGBTQ+ Travel Association (IGLTA)**, and **Global Sustainable Tourism Council (GSTC)**, provide valuable resources and best practices for serving diverse traveler groups. Engaging with these associations allows hospitality and tourism businesses to stay informed about global travel trends, learn about cultural competence, and connect with networks that promote diversity, equity, and inclusion in tourism.

Accor's Commitment to Sustainability and Diversity with GSTC

Accor is a member of the **Global Sustainable Tourism Council (GSTC)** and has committed to adopting sustainable practices across its properties. The company's sustainability initiatives align with GSTC's standards, which include environmental protection, community support, and cultural preservation. By partnering with GSTC and promoting responsible tourism, Accor positions itself as a brand that meets the needs of eco-conscious travelers while supporting local cultures and communities.

Preparing Staff for Global Cultural Competence

Cultural competence in hospitality and tourism is not just about policies and services; it's about people. To prepare for a global market, it is essential to invest in staff training and development that equips team members to serve a diverse range of guests with respect, empathy, and understanding.

1. Cross-Cultural Training and Sensitivity Workshops

Providing cross-cultural training is key to preparing staff to engage with guests from various backgrounds. This training should cover topics such as cultural customs, religious practices, communication styles, and how to provide personalized service based on individual needs. Workshops on unconscious bias and cultural humility are also effective in helping staff recognize and address their own biases, ensuring that all guests are treated with respect and dignity.

2. Building a Multilingual Workforce

Having a multilingual workforce is a valuable asset for any hospitality and tourism business serving a global market. Employing staff who can communicate in guests' native languages not only improves service but also creates a welcoming environment for international travelers. Hospitality and tourism businesses should encourage language training, provide resources for learning new languages, and seek to hire multilingual employees for guest-facing roles.

IHG's Cultural Training for Front-Line Staff

InterContinental Hotels Group (IHG) provides its front-line staff with training on cultural competence, language skills, and service excellence. Through its **Diversity & Inclusion Academy**, IHG equips its team members with the skills and knowledge needed to provide outstanding service to guests from diverse backgrounds. This focus on staff development ensures that guests receive personalized, culturally aware service at every touchpoint of their stay.

Conclusion: Embracing a Global Future with Cultural Competence

The future of the hospitality and tourism industry is global, diverse, and ever-changing. To prepare for this future, hospitality and tourism businesses must embrace cultural competence at every level—understanding and respecting the unique needs of their guests, delivering personalized and authentic experiences, and building partnerships that support diversity, equity, and inclusion.

By investing in staff training, enhancing guest services through technology, and partnering with local and global networks, hospitality and tourism businesses can not only meet the demands of a global market but also create enriching and memorable experiences that reflect the beauty of the world's diverse cultures. The journey to becoming culturally competent is ongoing, but it is a journey that holds immense rewards for both businesses and the travelers they serve.

References:

1. **WTTC and UNWTO Travel Trends Reports** – Insights into global travel patterns and emerging markets.

2. **Marriott's Bonvoy Moments Initiative** – Curated experiential travel opportunities.

3. **IHG's Green Engage Program** – Sustainable hospitality practices.

4. **Accor's Cultural Adaptation Strategies** – Tailored guest experiences across regions.

5. **Hilton Honors App and Digital Key** – Enhancing global guest experience through technology.

6. **Hyatt's Find Experiences** – Culturally immersive activities for global travelers.

7. **IHG's Diversity & Inclusion Academy** – Cross-cultural training for front-line staff.

CHAPTER 10

PITBULL CONVENTION & CONFERENCE SERVICES: LEADING THE WAY

As diversity and cultural competence become increasingly recognized as vital elements of success in the hospitality and tourism industry, the need for expert consulting services to guide organizations through this transformation has never been greater. Pitbull Convention and Conference Services (*Pitbull CCS*) an African American-owned and operated firm, prioritizes uplifting communities of color while offering strategic solutions to help hospitality and tourism businesses embrace and understand diversity, build cultural competence, and create meaningful experiences for diverse clients and guests. In this chapter, I will explore how **Pitbull Convention and Conference Services** is uniquely positioned to drive change in the industry and serve as a leader in diversity, equity, and inclusion consulting.

The Vision and Mission of Pitbull Convention and Conference Services

As an African American-owned and operated firm, **Pitbull Convention and Conference Services** has a unique perspective on the importance of diversity, equity, and inclusion in the hospitality and tourism industry. Our mission is *to assist organizations in creating inclusive environments and experiences that reflect the rich diversity of their clients and communities, with a specific focus on amplifying the voices of communities of color.* Pitbull CCS is driven by the understanding that creating spaces that honor all cultures and identities not only improves business performance but also fosters a sense of belonging for guests and staff alike.

How we got our name: One of our clients hired us to source, manage, and handle a large Convention in Orlando, Florida. From the moment of engaging with the sales staff to the Pre-Con, we were on top of everything. I believe *"God is in the detail!"* From amenities put into the VIP rooms, meetings and breakout sessions, Food & Beverage functions, restaurant and room service engagement, front desk check-in, flipping of rooms for meeting, etc. – I was there to monitor and make sure everything was done right for our client and those attending the Convention (550+). Once all guests had checked out and the event was over, my clients said, *"Dr. Montee, you handled this like a pitbull, not letting one thing fall apart."* I thought to myself, what a great name for a company. I think you can visualize how intense I was at making sure the ball was not dropped at all. Thus, a new company was formed.

Back in 1995, I read a book during undergrad that sticks with me to this day, and I use it in how I work, **"The Pursuit of WOW!"** by *Tom Peters*. He was at that time, America's customer service guru and I wanted to know what it took to get to that level. I wanted all of my clients to say, *"WOW Dr. Montee, that was amazing!"*

Another book I read was, **"The Personal Touch"** by *Terrie Williams*. She reminds those of us in business to remember one key fact about a potential or current client (*i.e., birthday, anniversary, graduation, tragic loss, death of parent, spouse, friend, child, etc.*) and reach out to them on or around that day to show you were listening and heard them and took note of something significant in their life. I listen from the moment we say "hello" to find a personal touch and build the relationship from there. Hospitality and tourism businesses have to get in the practice of listening for personal touch moments, especially cross culturally. These two books **and mine** should be must reads for leaders and managers in the hospitality and tourism business.

Drawing on decades of experience in meeting and event planning, destination management, and diversity training, we offer a comprehensive suite of services designed to help clients achieve their goals. By focusing on the needs of communities of color and marginalized communities (*i.e., LGBTQ+, Individuals with Disabilities, Etc.*), we provide consulting that ensures authentic representation, cultural awareness, and equitable practices that go beyond surface-level inclusion.

Case Study: Transforming Guest Experiences through Cultural Competence

One of Pitbull CCS' most impactful projects involved working with an organization in the Southeastern United States to enhance its cultural competence and guest experiences. The organization was preparing to host an international conference with attendees from over 50 countries, each bringing their own cultural customs, dietary preferences, and communication styles. Recognizing the importance of creating an inclusive environment for all guests, the organization engaged Pitbull CCS to guide its preparations.

1. Needs Assessment and Training

The first task was to conduct a needs assessment doing a deep dive into the specific cultural needs of the diverse communities that would be attending the conference. We placed a strong emphasis on prioritizing the experiences of communities of color and their cultural norms and values. This meant not only identifying dietary preferences and service needs but also understanding how cultural and historical context plays a role in their expectations and comfort.

Developing a Training Module Focused on Cultural Sensitivity and Service Customization:

We developed a training for the organization that included modules on understanding cultural nuances in guest interactions, offering inclusive dining options, and providing language support. Pitbull's team emphasized the importance of recognizing non-verbal cues and communication styles that vary across cultures, as well as respecting religious practices and dietary restrictions. By the end of the training, staff members reported feeling more confident in their ability to provide a welcoming experience to attendees from all backgrounds, with particular attention to cultural sensitivity toward communities of color.

2. Adapting Services for a Global Audience

Pitbull CCS also worked with the organization to incorporate services for an international audience. This included offering translated materials for attendees, providing safe spaces for prayer and meditation, and collaborating with local caterers to ensure that Halal, Kosher, Vegetarian, and Gluten-Free options were available. The organization sourced culturally relevant entertainment and programming that reflected the diverse backgrounds of its attendees, enhancing their overall attendee experience. This was probably the most fun, because people from different parts of the world knew the organization had them in mind from the onset of the planning process.

Results and Feedback: The conference was a success, with guests praising the organization for its attention to cultural details and their ability to create an inclusive and respectful environment. The positive feedback resulted in increased members for the organization, drawing on their ability to incorporate cultural competence in all aspects of the convention planning and management process.

Driving Change through Inclusive Event Planning and Marketing

Another area where **Pitbull Convention and Conference Services** has made a significant impact is in inclusive event planning, management, and marketing strategies. For many Hotels, CVBs, DMOs, and event venues, the challenge lies not just in attracting diverse clients but also in ensuring the events they host are designed with inclusivity in mind, particularly for communities that have been historically underrepresented or marginalized.

Case Study: A Destination Marketing Campaign with an Inclusive Lens

Pitbull Convention and Conference Services was contracted to work with a DMO in the Midwest to launch a marketing campaign aimed at attracting travelers from diverse cultural backgrounds, with a focus on communities of color. The DMO wanted to promote its city as a welcoming and inclusive destination for conventions, family reunions, and cultural festivals, but its existing marketing materials did not reflect the diversity of the audiences it hoped to reach (*i.e., no people of color on materials, website, or in leadership*).

1. Inclusive Marketing Audit (IMA)

At the onset, Pitbull CCS conduced an audit of the DMO's existing marketing materials, including brochures, social media content, website, and advertisements. The IMA revealed that the imagery and language used were not representative of the city's diverse communities and did not resonate with multicultural travelers, particularly Black and Brown communities. The DMO also lacked partnerships with cultural organizations and community groups that could help amplify its message of inclusion.

2. Developing an Inclusive Marketing Strategy

To address these challenges, Pitbull CCS helped the DMO update its existing marketing strategy to center on inclusion. This included creating content that highlighted the city's cultural events, diverse neighborhoods, and multicultural attractions. The DMO also partnered with local influencers and community leaders from communities of color to promote the city's offerings authentically.

Results: The revamped marketing campaign led to a notable increase in interest from diverse travel groups and organizations looking for event venues. The DMO's website traffic increased by over 30%, with a significant portion of new visitors coming from markets *previously underrepresented* in the city's tourism base. Additionally, the partnerships formed with local cultural organizations helped establish the DMO as a trusted ally in promoting diversity, equity, and inclusion, particularly among Black, Latinx, and other communities of color.

Supporting Diverse Supplier Development

In addition to consulting on guest experiences and marketing, **Pitbull Convention and Conference Services** also assists clients in developing diverse supplier programs. As an African American-owned business, Pitbull has a deep commitment to supporting other minority-owned businesses, women-owned enterprises, and local vendors. By working with these suppliers, hospitality and tourism companies can strengthen their supply chains, contribute to economic development, and ensure that their services reflect a commitment to diversity.

Case Study: Building a Diverse Supplier Network for a Boutique Hotel Chain

A boutique hotel chain approached **Pitbull Convention and Conference Services** for support in building a supplier diversity program that prioritized partnerships with communities of color. The chain aimed to increase its use of local and diverse suppliers for its food and beverage offerings, event services, and guest amenities, while also ensuring that these partnerships aligned with its brand values and guest needs. This required relationship building since they were a boutique hotel with a specific focus on the guest experience they wanted to provide.

1. Supplier Diversity Framework Development

Pitbull CCS conducted an assessment to determine if a supplier network existed that was operational. They had a list of companies to call when they had certain guests in-house but no demographics or description of the company, all the services they could provide, key contact information, etc. We worked with the hotel to formalize a supplier diversity framework with an established criteria for selecting and evaluating potential suppliers. This framework prioritized working with businesses owned by entrepreneurs of color, women, veterans, LGBTQ+ individuals, and those from underrepresented communities. Pitbull also facilitated conversations and opportunities with local minority-owned suppliers who could meet the hotel chain's standards for quality and service. These systems were replicated at other properties owned by this hotel chain. New policies and procedures were developed on how to identify local supplies; forms were designed and made fillable online; registration packets for becoming a supplier were created; and training for supplies who had never engaged a procurement system was developed.

2. Creating Long-Term Partnerships

To foster long-term relationships with diverse suppliers, Pitbull CCS organized networking events, luncheons, and business development workshops where suppliers could meet hotel representatives, learn about upcoming procurement opportunities, learn the process of becoming a supplier, and receive feedback on how to improve their services. This approach not only built strong partnerships but also helped suppliers grow their businesses and contribute to the economic development of their communities, particularly communities of color.

Results: The hotel chain successfully increased its use of diverse suppliers by 40%, resulting in more authentic and localized guest experiences, positive community engagement, and a stronger commitment to diversity within its operations.

Empowering Leadership and Policy Development for Inclusivity

Pitbull Convention and Conference Services knows and understands that lasting change in diversity and cultural competence requires leadership commitment and sound policies. As an African American-owned firm, we bring a unique perspective to this work, advocating for policies and practices that encourage hospitality and tourism leaders to support communities of color and create equitable opportunities within the industry.

Case Study: Leadership Development for Inclusive Event Planning

A company in the Northeast sought Pitbull CCS' help in training its leadership team on the principles of inclusive event planning. It's one thing to say, *"All Are Welcome!"* and an entirely different narrative when only non-people of color are doing the welcoming. The company was transitioning to a new strategic plan with a focus on attracting events that catered to diverse communities and cultures. However, many of its leaders were unfamiliar with inclusive planning principles and needed guidance on how to develop and execute the new strategy effectively, with a particular emphasis on engaging communities of color.

1. Executive Training and Inclusive Policy Development

We led executive training sessions focused on understanding diversity in event planning, identifying potential barriers to inclusivity, and developing policies that support diverse hiring, vendor selection, and guest experiences. Leaders and managers participated in role-playing exercises, case studies, and facilitated discussions to gain practical insights into how they could create more inclusive events and policies that centered around Black and Brown communities.

2. Policy Implementation and Community Engagement

The company's leadership team worked with Pitbull CCS to draft policies that supported diversity in their event planning processes. These policies included measures for inclusive hiring, accessible event design, representation in marketing and advertising materials, and collaboration with diverse community partners to enhance the experiences of those attending events. The company also hosted community forums (*refreshments were served*) to gather input on how to best serve their city's diverse population.

Results: The company's leadership acquired a deeper understanding of inclusive event planning which led to a series of successful culturally themed events that attracted a broader range of attendees and promoted positive community relations. The company's commitment to inclusivity established it as a leader in the local community and helped to increase its event bookings among diverse organizations and cultural groups, particularly those led by or serving communities of color.

Conclusion: The Value of an African American-Owned Consulting Firm in Leading Cultural Competence and Diversity

The work of **Pitbull Convention and Conference Services** demonstrates the transformative power of diversity, equity, and inclusion within the hospitality and tourism industry. As an African American-owned and operated consulting firm, Pitbull CCS not only offers expertise but also a strong commitment to uplifting communities of color. Our approach centers on enhancing cultural competence, developing inclusive marketing strategies, building diverse supplier programs, and empowering leadership to make equitable decisions. Through these tailored services, we help our clients improve their operations while becoming true advocates for diversity, equity, and inclusion.

That said, we're not the only African American consulting firm providing these services—there are many firms with equal, if not greater, talent, experience, and skills. It's surprising how often people express that they didn't even know companies like ours existed. Each of us brings a unique focus to the hospitality and tourism industry, and I encourage you to seek out a consulting firm—whether it's Pitbull CCS or another—that can help you strengthen your diversity, equity, and inclusion efforts. *After all, you are tracking your progress, right?*

As the industry continues to evolve, the role of consulting firms like ours becomes increasingly vital. **Pitbull Convention and Conference Services** is dedicated to guiding hotels, CVBs, DMOs, event venues, tourism companies, and others through the challenges and opportunities of cultural competence and diversity. We work closely with our clients to ensure that every guest experience is meaningful, every event is inclusive, and every business practice is equitable.

At Pitbull CCS, our core principle is forming meaningful and authentic relationships, where open, honest conversations can take place without fear of offending one another. Our mission is to make sure that people of color and other underrepresented groups—such as LGBTQ+ individuals and those with mobility challenges—feel seen, understood, and valued at every event or function we are privileged to be a part of, even if we never meet them personally.

References:

1. **Organization Transformation Project** – Feedback from international guests and results of training and service adaptation, with a focus on communities of color.

2. **Corporate Inclusive Marketing Campaign** – Outcomes from the inclusive marketing strategy and increased engagement, particularly among Black, Latinx, and other communities of color.

3. **Supplier Diversity Success for Boutique Hotel Chain** – Details of increased partnerships with diverse suppliers from communities of color.

4. **Leadership Development and Policy Implementation for Northeast Company** – Positive impact on inclusive event planning and community engagement, focusing on policies that benefit communities of color.

CONCLUSION

CHARTING THE PATH FORWARD FOR AN INCLUSIVE HOSPITALITY & TOURISM INDUSTRY

The hospitality and tourism industry is uniquely positioned to bring people together, transcend cultural boundaries, and create experiences that celebrate the diversity of human life. Throughout this book, I have explored how diversity, equity, and inclusion (DEI) are not only social imperatives but also crucial business drivers that enhance guest experiences, strengthen brand loyalty, and foster economic empowerment. As we conclude, we will revisit the key takeaways, outline actionable next steps for hospitality and tourism businesses, and emphasize the role that consulting firms like **Pitbull Convention and Conference Services** can play in shaping a more inclusive and culturally competent future.

Reflecting on the Journey Toward Diversity and Cultural Competence

Our journey began by examining the historical context of diversity in the hospitality and tourism industry, highlighting both progress and persistent challenges. The history of segregation, exclusion, and underrepresentation has cast a long shadow over the industry, creating systemic barriers for people of color, women, LGBTQ+ individuals, and those with disabilities. Yet, as we explored, there has been a growing awareness and effort to challenge these norms, elevate diverse voices, and create spaces where all travelers feel welcomed and valued.

We also delved into cultural competence—its definition, significance, and best practices. It became clear that cultural competence is not about box-checking or token gestures; it's about developing an understanding of different cultures, actively listening to guests' needs, and fostering environments that are sensitive and respectful to all backgrounds. It's about building an industry where diversity is celebrated, representation is prioritized, and equity is embedded into every aspect of business operations.

Key Takeaways for Creating an Inclusive Hospitality Industry

1. **Diversity Drives Innovation and Profitability**:

Embracing diverse leadership, teams, and perspectives fosters creativity, improves decision-making, and enhances business performance. A commitment to diversity, equity, and inclusion is not only ethically right but also financially beneficial, as diverse organizations are better equipped to serve a global market and attract new customer bases.

2. **Representation Matters at Every Level**:

Representation is key to authentic hospitality and tourism experiences. When leadership reflects the diversity of its workforce and customers, decisions are made with a fuller understanding of guest needs. Representation extends to marketing, event planning, guest services, and supplier partnerships—ensuring that every touchpoint is inclusive and welcoming.

3. **Cultural Competence is Essential to Personalization**:

Personalizing guest experiences is at the heart of hospitality and tourism, and cultural competence is the foundation of personalization. Understanding and respecting cultural differences in communication, dietary preferences, religious practices, and customs allow businesses to create memorable and meaningful experiences for their guests.

4. **Inclusive Event Planning and Marketing Strategies**:

Inclusive event planning requires attention to cultural details, such as accessible spaces, diverse food options, language support, and culturally relevant entertainment. Marketing strategies should authentically represent diverse communities, collaborations with creatives from underrepresented backgrounds, and avoid reinforcing stereotypes or tokenism.

5. **Partnerships Enhance Diversity and Local Engagement**:

Forming partnerships with local cultural organizations, diverse suppliers, and advocacy groups enhances cultural competence and strengthens community ties. These partnerships allow businesses to serve their guests better while supporting local economies and promoting equity.

The Role of Pitbull Convention and Conference Services in Leading Change

As an African American-owned consulting firm, **Pitbull Convention and Conference Services** plays a pivotal role in promoting DEI across the hospitality and tourism industry. With a focus on prioritizing communities of color, Pitbull CCS provides consulting services that support organizations in building inclusive environments, developing diverse marketing strategies, and fostering cultural competence at every level. Our three-prong strategy:

1. **Elevating Communities of Color and Underrepresented Groups**: Pitbull CCS' mission is to elevate the voices and experiences of communities of color and historically marginalized groups. By working directly with Hotels, CVBs, DMOs, and

Event Venues; Pitbull CCS helps organizations create policies and practices that not only attract diverse clients but also create equitable opportunities for employees, suppliers, and guests.

2. **Consulting Services that Foster Authentic Representation**: Pitbull CCS provides tailored consulting services to support clients in designing events, programs, and campaigns that reflect the diversity of the communities they serve (*or want to serve*). This includes conducting DEI audits, Internal Marketing Audits, training staff on cultural competence, building diverse supplier networks, and developing or providing feedback on marketing content that authentically represents multicultural perspectives.

3. **Policy Development and Leadership Empowerment**: Pitbull CCS emphasizes the importance of leadership commitment to DEI and works with clients to develop policies that prioritize inclusivity, equity, and representation. By guiding organizations in creating pathways for diverse leadership and building supportive workplace cultures, Pitbull CCS helps businesses move from intention to action.

Actionable Steps for Businesses Committed to DEI

To create lasting change and build an inclusive hospitality and tourism industry, businesses must take actionable steps that align with their DEI goals and values. Below are practical recommendations to help organizations chart their path forward:

1. Conduct a Diversity and Inclusion Assessment

Start by assessing your organization's current state of diversity, equity, and inclusion. Review hiring practices, guest services, supplier relationships, marketing materials, and policies to identify areas where improvements can be made. Consider bringing in a DEI consultant, to conduct a thorough audit and provide recommendations.

2. Set Measurable DEI Goals and Accountability Structures

Establish clear, measurable DEI goals that address diverse hiring, supplier diversity, inclusive marketing, community partnerships, and guest experiences. Create accountability structures, such as a Diversity, Equity, and Inclusion Council or DEI Scorecard, to track progress, measure outcomes, and ensure that leadership is responsible for advancing these goals.

3. Invest in Cultural Competence Training for All Staff

Provide ongoing training on cultural competence for all staff members, including front-line employees, managers, and executives. Training should cover topics such as cultural awareness, cross-cultural communication, unconscious bias, and personalized service for diverse guests. Encourage staff to develop cultural humility, empathy, and an openness to learning from diverse perspectives.

4. Prioritize Representation in Marketing and Guest Services

Ensure your marketing materials reflect the diversity of your guests and authentically represent different communities. Work with diverse creatives, photographers, and influencers to tell genuine stories that resonate with multicultural travelers. Tailor guest services to meet the needs of diverse groups, from offering multilingual support to providing culturally relevant amenities.

5. Build and Maintain Diverse Partnerships and Community Engagement

Actively seek partnerships with diverse suppliers, local cultural organizations, minority business associations, and advocacy groups. Support community events, engage in local philanthropy, and participate in programs that promote social impact and economic development for underrepresented communities.

Envisioning a Diverse and Inclusive Future

The future of hospitality and tourism is diverse, global, and interconnected. It is a future where guests from all backgrounds hope to find hotels, spaces, and experiences that welcome, respect, and celebrate all of who they are. It is a future where leadership teams are diverse, services are culturally competent, and experiences are designed to create a sense of belonging for all travelers.

By embracing diversity and cultural competence, I believe the hospitality and tourism industry can unlock the power of human connection, foster richer travel experiences, and build communities where **every person** feels seen, heard, and valued. The work of creating a diverse and inclusive hospitality and tourism industry is ongoing, but it is a journey worth pursuing—one that holds the promise of a better, more equitable world for everyone.

I wish all of those who have read to the end absolute success in building your hospitality and tourism business. *You got this!* – as an industry, we are stronger together when we work hand in hand for diversity, equity, and inclusion on all levels and in all sectors of the industry.

Final Reflections and Resources for Continued Learning:

1. **DEI Consulting and Leadership Development** – Exploring the role of consulting firms in promoting diversity, equity, and inclusion.

2. **Industry Reports on Travel Demographics and Trends** – Understanding how global travel patterns are shifting and the needs of diverse travelers.

3. **Best Practices for Culturally Competent Service** – Resources on training programs, guest personalization, and cultural awareness in hospitality.

4. **Community Engagement and Supplier Diversity** – Building partnerships and economic opportunities that support diverse and local communities.

5. **Global Travel Associations and Cultural Competence** – Engaging with organizations that support DEI and sustainable tourism.

ABOUT THE AUTHOR

Dr. LaMont "Montee" Evans is the *President/CEO* of **Pitbull Convention & Conference Services, LLC**, Its mission is to assist organizations in creating inclusive environments and experiences that reflect the rich diversity of their clients and communities, with a specific focus on amplifying the voices of communities of color. **Pitbull Convention & Conference Services, LLC** is driven by the understanding that creating spaces that honor all cultures and identities not only improves business performance but also fosters a sense of belonging for guests and staff alike.

Dr. Evans' passion for fairness, equity, and inclusion has driven him to work tirelessly for marginalized and underserved communities across the globe. His efforts have earned him invitations to speak at prestigious conferences worldwide, including the United Nations General Assembly and the World Health Assembly in Geneva. In recognition of his contributions, he was awarded an Honorary Doctorate of Letters from American Bible University in 2022.

Born and raised in St. Louis, Missouri, Dr. Evans has travels extensively and continues to champion the causes of those without a voice, ensuring that their stories and needs are heard and addressed on local, national, and international platforms.

For more information on consulting or to hire Dr. Evans to speak at a conference, event, function, conduct a workshop/training, please visit www.pitbullccservices.com.

ACKNOWLEDGMENTS

First and foremost, I would like to express my deepest gratitude to **International Masons and Eastern Stars** for trusting me to manage multiple large conventions over the years. To the many National, Regional, State and Local Leaders who put their trust in me and my suggestions - your unwavering faith in my abilities has allowed me to grow and thrive in this field. Thank you.

A very special thank you to **James O. Dogan**, *Past Supreme President/CEO* – **International Masons** who gave me my first opportunity 14 years ago right here in Atlanta, Georgia to help him make a National Convention better. Your belief in me set the foundation for everything that followed, and I am forever grateful for that chance. May God bless you and **Mama Minnie**.

To my favorite brother, **James Evans**: Your watchful eye, both inside and outside this book, ensured that every detail represents the quality and integrity an Evans' product should have. Thank you for your love, support and guidance throughout this entire process. You told me at a very young age, *"Evans means strong, look it up in the dictionary."* I believed you then and now I know if it doesn't, it should be defined as such. I love you with my whole heart.

I would also like to thank **International Masons' State of Florida** leaders and members for the trust you've placed in me over the years. In particular, my heartfelt appreciation goes to **Bobbie J. Meeks**, **Christine Hayes**, **Alex "Rico" Dixon**, and **Khandia Smith** for your encouragement, faith, and partnership. Your belief in my work has been instrumental in bringing this vision to life. Also, those members and leaders within the State of Florida who have sought me out for guidance, direction, and conversation – my heart is full.

To the many African American men and women I have met at tradeshows over the last 10+ years, who generously shared your stories, thank you. Your experiences have deeply shaped my understanding of the challenges and triumphs within our industry. I consider each conversation sacred.

A special thanks to the CVB & **DMO** sales professionals from communities of color and the LGBTQ+ community who opened up about the internal struggles you face by sometimes being the only one in the room. Your courage and persistence in navigating those spaces, and fighting those battles have inspired me, and I hope this book honors your stories and contributions. Equity will come sooner as long as we keep on pushing.

Lastly, thank you to everyone who has supported me along this journey. This book reflects the collective belief, support, and trust you have all placed in me. I didn't get here by myself and thanks to the many whose name may not be in this book but who also helped to make me who and what I am today.

*****

www.ingramcontent.com/pod-product-compliance
Lightning Source LLC
Chambersburg PA
CBHW050649160426
43194CB00010B/1869